5 INGREDIENTS

MEDITERRANEAN DIET

COOKBOOK

Finally Achieve the Perfect Balance Between Taste, Convenience, and Health. Discover Healthy Mediterranean Recipes, Ready in Minutes, With 30-Day Meal Plan Included

Eliana Nikos

TABLE OF CONTENTS

4.2 5-Ingredient Salad Recipes   56

4.3 5-Ingredient Veggie Recipes   62

CHAPTER 5: SAUCES AND DIPS   69

5.1 5-Ingredient Sauces and Dips   70

CHAPTER 6: SEAFOOD, MEAT AND POULTRY DISHES 77

6.1 5-Ingredient Seafood Recipes 78

6.2 5-Ingredient Meat and Poultry Recipes 84

CHAPTER 7: DESSERTS 91

7.1 5-Ingredient Dessert Recipes 92

INTRODUCTION

Welcome to a journey that is much more than just a way of eating it's a transformative lifestyle embraced along the sun-splashed Mediterranean coast. Picture yourself savoring a meal that is as nourishing as it is delightful, crafted with the vibrant colors and heart-healthy ingredients typical of Mediterranean cuisine. Each bite not only tantalizes your taste buds but also brings you closer to a world where food is a joyful celebration of life.

In writing *5 Ingredients Mediterranean Diet Cookbook*, I invite you to discover how simple and satisfying this ancient, time-tested dietary pattern can be. The Mediterranean diet has been cherished for centuries, not only for its health benefits but also for its emphasis on variety, flavor, and the pleasure of sharing meals with loved ones. However, embracing this eating style doesn't require hours in the kitchen or hard-to-find ingredients. On the contrary, my approach simplifies Mediterranean cooking, breaking it down to the essentials five key ingredients that ensure each dish is approachable but still delightfully delicious.

Through these pages, you will learn that eating healthily doesn't have to be complicated. Imagine dishes that combine fresh vegetables, fruits, lean proteins, and heart-healthy fats all coming together in perfect harmony, with minimal fuss and maximum flavor. Whether you're a busy professional, a parent juggling family schedules, or someone simply looking for a healthful twist on home-cooked meals, this book is designed for you.

Join me as we embark on this flavorful adventure, embracing the Mediterranean way of life where every meal is an opportunity to slow down, relish the moment, and nourish not just the body, but also the soul. You'll find that adopting this diet can be effortless, enjoyable, and incredibly rewarding. Here's to your health, happiness, and a new, vibrant way of eating!

WELCOME TO THE MEDITERRANEAN LIFESTYLE

Imagine walking along a sun-kissed coastal path in Southern Italy or Greece, the air rich with the scents of rosemary, the sea, and freshly baked bread. This vision captures the essence of the Mediterranean lifestyle, a rich tapestry of tastes and traditions that is about much more than the foods you put on your plate. It is a philosophy of life, centered on balance, wellness, and the enjoyment of every moment. As we embark on this journey together through this book, I invite you to understand and adopt this beautiful lifestyle, not only through its cuisines but also through its deeply rooted cultural practices.

The Mediterranean lifestyle is a testament to living well where eating is an experience of joy and celebration. It encompasses late afternoon meals with family, leisurely strolls through bustling markets, and the generous act of sharing. It's in the old Greek proverb, **"Good food and good**

company heal the soul," that we find the central pillar of the Mediterranean way of life. Here food is not just sustenance; it's a way to bond, to appreciate the bountiful nature, and to nourish both body and spirit. This holistic approach to life emphasizes not only physical well-being but also mental and emotional health, integrating all into a seamless, vibrant lifestyle that many find appealing.

One fundamental aspect of this lifestyle is the diet, which is renowned for its health benefits, particularly heart health and longevity. The Mediterranean diet is predominantly plant-based, rich in vegetables, fruits, whole grains, and healthy fats from olive oil, nuts, and fish. It's a diet that mirrors the natural resources and bright flavors of the region and is minimalist yet abundant in variety. Simplicity is at the heart of the Mediterranean kitchen. Dishes emphasize fresh and few ingredients, letting the natural flavors shine, which aligns perfectly with the principles of this cookbook.

But it's not just about the food. The lifestyle also promotes physical activity woven into daily life be it farming, walking, or cycling as a natural part of existence rather than a scheduled chore. There is also a profound reverence for rest; siestas are a famous example of this, providing a midday pause that supports productivity and vitality.

Furthermore, the Mediterranean lifestyle embraces a set of values that includes warmth, hospitality, and a strong sense of community. Meals are often communal, leisurely, and centered around conversation and connection. This communal nature supports psychological well-being and aligns with the blue zones principles, where strong social ties are crucial for longevity.

Another characteristic that defines Mediterranean living is the connection with nature. From the cultivation of olive trees and vineyards to fishing along the shores of the Adriatic, this lifestyle encourages a harmonious relationship with the environment. Menus are seasonal, with a natural cycle dictating what is grown and when it is best to eat it. This not only makes for tastier meals but also lessens the ecological footprint, fostering sustainability.

Seasonality leads to another significant aspect sustainability and waste reduction. The Mediterranean way is resourceful, utilizing the entirety of each ingredient, be it in cooking or in preserving food for future use. This not only reduces waste but also enhances flavors, often seen in the sun-dried tomatoes of Italy or the preserved lemons of Northern Africa.

In essence, adopting the Mediterranean lifestyle means to slow down, savor each moment, and respect the gifts of nature. It teaches us to listen to our bodies, to feed them wholesome, colorful food, and to build our meals and days around what is both sustaining and delightful. It invites us to find joy in simplicity and sustainability while fostering connections with family and friends over shared meals.

So, as we delve deeper into the recipes and meal plans in this book, remember that each dish is more than a simple combination of ingredients. It is a celebration of life's simple pleasures and a step toward well-being, longevity, and harmony. Here within these pages, you will find more than just food; you will discover a new way of seeing the world and your place within it. The Mediterranean diet is not a trend; it's a centuries-old tradition that has stood the test of time, one that can enrich your life in immeasurable ways if you let it. Embrace this journey with an open heart, and let the vibrant textures and flavors guide you to a healthier, happier lifestyle. Welcome to the Mediterranean lifestyle a beautiful, delicious, and nutritious life awaits.

THE BENEFITS OF A MEDITERRANEAN DIET

Dive into the heart of the Mediterranean diet and you'll find a cornucopia of benefits ranging from enhanced physical health to improved mental well-being. This nourishing approach to eating, deeply ingrained in the cultural practices of regions like Greece, Italy, and Spain, is celebrated worldwide not only for its delicious flavors but also for its numerous health benefits, substantiated by decades of research.

Crucially, the Mediterranean diet has gained acclaim from the medical community for its ability to bolster heart health. Rich in olive oil, nuts, and fatty fish, it provides a balanced intake of omega-3 fatty acids and monounsaturated fats, which are known to reduce inflammation and decrease the risk of chronic diseases, particularly cardiovascular disorders. Studies consistently highlight how this diet lowers bad cholesterol levels, thereby reducing the risk of heart disease by enhancing the health of arteries and promoting a healthier blood lipid profile. Dive deeper into any story from the Mediterranean region, and you'll likely hear testimonials of longevity and heart health that accompany this dietary pattern.

Beyond heart health, the Mediterranean diet offers protective benefits against a myriad of chronic conditions. Its emphasis on whole grains, legumes, and vegetables equips the body with a treasure trove of fiber, vitamins, and minerals. These components play a crucial role in digestion, help regulate blood sugar levels, and support a healthy gut biome, which is pivotal in preventing type 2 diabetes and maintaining an overall healthy metabolism.

Cognitive benefits also stand out among the advantages of this diet. Rich in antioxidants and healthy fats, it supports brain function and combats cognitive decline, making it a valuable ally against age-related cognitive diseases such as Alzheimer's. Visualize the elderly of the Mediterranean regions many maintain sharp minds and vibrant lifestyles well into their older years, reflecting the diet's long-term benefits on brain health.

Cancer prevention is yet another noteworthy benefit. The diet's rich profiles in antioxidants, found abundantly in fruits and vegetables, help neutralize harmful free radicals that can cause oxidative stress and lead to cancerous changes in cells. Olive oil, a staple in the Mediterranean diet, is particularly potent in polyphenols, which have been shown to reduce the risk of breast and colon cancers.

Moreover, adopting this dietary pattern can lead to an improved quality of life and longevity. The Mediterranean diet emphasizes not just food, but the joy of meals enjoyed with family and friends. This social aspect encourages slower eating, mindful consumption, and overall, a more satisfying eating experience, reducing the common tendencies of overeating and its associated health risks.

Mental health, often overlooked in discussions about diet, receives a boost from the Mediterranean way of eating. Research suggests that the diet's high intake of vegetables, fruits, nuts, and fish correlates with a lower incidence of depression. These foods boost serotonin levels, a neurotransmitter responsible for feelings of well-being and happiness, thus supporting overall mental health.

In the realm of weight management, the Mediterranean diet proves to be a sustainable choice. Unlike restrictive diets, which can lead to yo-yo dieting and emotional eating, the Mediterranean diet offers a plethora of flavorful and satisfying options. It encourages portion control and emphasizes quality over quantity, promoting healthier lifestyle choices that lead to natural weight loss and maintenance without the deprivation and struggles associated with other diets.

Furthermore, the anti-inflammatory effects of the diet contribute to reducing the risk of autoimmune diseases and improving conditions such as rheumatoid arthritis and psoriasis. These benefits stem from the diet's rich supply of anti-inflammatory nutrients found in olive oil, leafy greens, nuts, and fatty fish.

The environmental impact, though a broader benefit, is significant. The Mediterranean diet favors seasonal, local, and plant-based foods, reducing reliance on processed foods and heavy meat consumption, contributing to lower carbon emissions and less strain on our environment. Embracing this diet means taking a step toward sustainable living, respecting the earth while nourishing oneself.

Ultimately, as you weave the vibrant threads of the Mediterranean diet into your daily eating habits, you embrace a fuller, richer approach to life. It's an all-encompassing embrace of food, family, and well-being that nourishes the soul as much as the body, demonstrating that the truest form of dieting is not deprivation but celebration of life done in harmony with nature's rhythms and human traditions. Here, at the confluence of taste, health, and pleasure, the Mediterranean diet stands as a beacon of holistic living and wellness.

Embarking on a culinary journey with the *5 Ingredients Mediterranean Diet Cookbook* is like discovering a treasured family recipe book, passed down through generations. Whether you're a seasoned chef or a beginner in the kitchen, this cookbook is designed to be your companion in crafting delicious, healthy meals with ease. The essence of Mediterranean cooking is encapsulated in its simplicity and reliance on high-quality ingredients, making it perfectly suited for anyone looking to infuse their diet with the flavors of this sun-rich region.

The structure and approach of this cookbook are tailored to encourage a seamless experience in your kitchen. Each recipe leverages five essential ingredients, ensuring that you maximize flavor without complexity. This is an invitation to streamline your cooking processes and focus on what truly matters: pure, simple, mouthwatering dishes that bring health and pleasure to your table.

Begin by familiarizing yourself with the format of this book. Each chapter focuses on a distinctive meal course or component of the Mediterranean diet from sunrise-fueled breakfasts and hearty soups to rich, indulgent desserts. The recipes are laid out to guide you effortlessly through the process, whether you are rushing to prepare a weekday dinner or leisurely crafting a meal for a gathering.

It's beneficial to start with the 'Essential Ingredients and Tools' section. Here, you will discover the pantry staples revered in Mediterranean kitchens. These ingredients form the backbone of the recipes in this book and understanding their importance and uses will enhance your cooking experience. Equally, knowledge of essential kitchen tools will equip you to handle any recipe in this cookbook and beyond effectively.

When approaching each recipe, notice the dual focus on simplicity and nutrition. The recipes are designed to be flexible, allowing room for substitutions based on dietary needs or what you have on hand. It's this adaptability that stands at the heart of Mediterranean cooking use what is fresh and available. Feel encouraged to experiment with herbs and spices to tailor dishes to your taste, creating a personal touch that resonates with your palate.

A significant feature to look out for in this book is the tips integrated into each recipe. These snippets of advice aim to enhance your cooking style, teaching you how to bring out robust flavors, improve your cooking techniques, or cut down on preparation time. The tips section is akin to having a knowledgeable friend guiding you through the intricacies of Mediterranean cuisine.

Moreover, the cookbook understands that not everyone has time to spend hours in the kitchen, which is why the cuisine's inherent simplicity is highlighted in the segment on 'Cooking Techniques for Quick and Healthy Meals'. This section supports your endeavor to prepare nutritious meals without the fuss, aligning with the busy lifestyles many lead today.

For those keen on embarking on a sustained healthy eating journey, the '30 Days Meal Plan' chapter provides a structured approach to incorporating Mediterranean meals into your daily life. This plan is more than a mere menu; it is designed to educate you on various combinations of food that maximize health benefits while keeping meals exciting.

Finally, the concluding sections of the book are crafted to inspire continuity in your Mediterranean diet adventure. It's here that the lifestyle aspect of the diet is woven together with nutritional advice to encourage a holistic approach to your new eating habits. You're not just following recipes; you're adopting a lifestyle that honors both tradition and health a sustainable practice that this book aims to instill and nurture in its readers.

As you turn each page of this cookbook, imagine yourself drifting through the Mediterranean coast, where cooking isn't just about feeding the body but nourishing the soul. With each recipe, you're invited to share in this cultural heritage, adopting a way of life that celebrates simplicity, health, and above all, joy in the everyday. Let this book be a gateway to transforming your meals and your life, creating a future richer in health and happiness, one delicious bite at a time.

TIPS FOR SUCCESS WITH 5-INGREDIENT RECIPES

Embracing the concept of 5-ingredient recipes within the Mediterranean diet isn't merely a culinary endeavor; it's a philosophy that simplifies cooking, shining a spotlight on quality and flavor. This approach facilitates a delightful exploration into the heart of Mediterranean cooking while enabling you to make the most out of every ingredient. Here, you'll find a guide imbued with tips to harness the power of simplicity, ensuring success as you blend minimalism with the rich tapestries of Mediterranean flavors.

First, understanding the essence of using fewer ingredients is vital. The magic in 5-ingredient recipes lies in their ability to showcase high-quality, fresh ingredients. Each component in a recipe carries weight and contributes significantly to the flavor profile of the dish. This means selecting the best possible ingredients is paramount. Whether it's sourcing the freshest vegetables from your local market, choosing high-quality olive oil, or using seafood caught on the same day, the quality of each ingredient should be non-negotiable.

The Mediterranean diet's reliance on fresh herbs and spices exemplifies how a dish can be tremendously enhanced without the clutter of numerous ingredients. Learning to use herbs like rosemary, basil, or mint effectively can transform a simple dish into a burst of sensory joy. They introduce not only flavor but also aromatics that turn a meal into a more dynamic experience. Experiment with growing your own herbs; even a small kitchen garden can provide you with fresh picks that elevate your cooking.

Another fundamental tip centers around mastering a few cooking techniques that highlight the inherent flavors of key ingredients. Sautéing, grilling, and roasting are all methods that, when done well, can boost the natural sweetness and richness of your food. For instance, roasting vegetables in a drizzle of olive oil and a sprinkle of sea salt can enhance their natural sugars and flavors, making them star components in any dish.

Besides focusing on ingredients and cooking methods, another tip for success with simple recipes is the art of seasoning. Mediterranean cuisine is not about heavy, complex seasoning but rather the strategic use of salt and pepper, along with key spices. Learn to season in layers add a little salt during cooking and a final adjustment just before serving. This method helps to amplify the flavors of the individual ingredients rather than overshadowing them.

Timing in cooking is also crucial particularly when dealing with few ingredients. Overcooking can wilt the vibrance of fresh produce and turn potentially succulent fish or meat into tough, dry bites. Keep a vigilant eye on cooking times and trust your senses. Often, the scent, look, and feel of the food can tell you more about when a dish is ready than the timer.

The importance of presentation should not be underestimated in any culinary tradition, especially in one that honors the visuals of its dishes as much as their tastes. In Mediterranean cuisine, the appeal of colorful vegetables, bright herbs, and glistening oils is part of the eating experience. When plating your food, consider the balance of colors and textures how the greens, reds, and oranges create a palette that is as pleasing to the eye as it is to the palate.

Embrace the idea of flexibility within the framework of your recipes. The Mediterranean diet is forgiving and adaptable, reflecting the seasons and availability of local produce. If you find yourself missing an ingredient, consider suitable substitutions that maintain the integrity of the dish. Such adaptability not only fosters creativity but also resilience in your cooking habits.

Planning ahead is likewise beneficial when working with minimal-ingredient meals. Since each ingredient plays a significant role, having everything on hand before you start cooking ensures a smooth, uninterrupted process. Take time before meals to prepare your ingredients washing, chopping, and measuring them out. This mise en place, or everything in its place, not only streamlines your cooking experience but also enhances your connection with the food as you prepare it.

Lastly, enjoy the process. The joy of Mediterranean cooking comes from more than the delicious results it's found in the rhythm of preparing food, the aromas that fill the kitchen, the textures of fresh ingredients under your hands, and the anticipation of sharing your creations with loved ones. Even with the simplest recipes, this journey from kitchen to table is an enriching tradition that nourishes both body and soul in the Mediterranean way.

With these tips and a spirit of curiosity and passion, the 5-ingredient recipes in this cookbook are not just meals but gateways to mastering the art of simple, satisfying, and healthy Mediterranean eating. Dive into each recipe with confidence, knowing that each dish offers a canvas on which to refine your culinary skills and enjoy the rich tapestry of flavors that this age-old dietary tradition has to offer.

ESSENTIAL INGREDIENTS AND TOOLS

Embarking on a Mediterranean cooking adventure begins with a pantry and kitchen equipped with a few essential ingredients and tools that epitomize the simplicity and richness of this celebrated cuisine. The beauty of the Mediterranean diet lies not just in its flavorful dishes but in its straightforward, unadulterated preparation methods that anyone, no matter their culinary skill level, can adopt and enjoy.

Let us explore the foundational elements that make up the cornerstone of Mediterranean cooking. These ingredients are vital, not just for their versatility, but for their ability to bring the authentic essence of Mediterranean flavors into your home.

Olive Oil

At the heart of every Mediterranean kitchen is olive oil, known affectionately as the liquid gold of the region due to its numerous health benefits and its central role in cooking. A high-quality extra virgin olive oil provides a robust foundation for dressings, marinades, cooking, and even finishing dishes with a drizzle right before serving. Its rich, fruity flavor and high content of monounsaturated fats make it indispensable not only for its taste but also for its heart-healthy benefits.

Fresh Vegetables

The vibrant bounty of fresh vegetables forms the colorful palette of the Mediterranean diet. Staples include leafy greens like spinach and kale; nightshades such as eggplants and tomatoes; and a variety of squashes and root vegetables. These are not just side dishes or afterthoughts but are central to the daily diet, celebrated for their flavors and nutritional value.

Whole Grains

Nutty, hearty whole grains like farro, bulgur, and barley regularly appear in Mediterranean meals. They are typically enjoyed in a naturally uncomplicated form, perhaps lightly seasoned or tossed with a splash of olive oil and lemon, allowing their intrinsic textures and flavors to shine through. These grains contribute fiber and important nutrients, playing a key role in digestive health and sustainable energy levels throughout the day.

Legumes

Beans and lentils are a protein-packed feature of the Mediterranean diet, offering both substance and texture to various dishes from soups to salads. Rich in fiber and low in fat, legumes are an excellent meat substitute, aligned with the diet's emphasis on plant-based eating and sustainability.

Nuts and Seeds

Almonds, pistachios, walnuts, and seeds like sesame are more than just snacks in the Mediterranean diet. They are integral to adding crunch and nutritional value to dishes, used creatively in everything from pestos and dips to salads and desserts.

Herbs and Spices

The Mediterranean palette of flavors is incomplete without the fresh and dried herbs and spices that season its dishes. Basil, oregano, rosemary, and thyme are just a few that might fill terracotta pots in a Mediterranean kitchen garden. These herbs not only provide flavorful accents but are also packed with antioxidants, showcasing the natural melding of flavor and health in the diet.

Equipping your kitchen with the right tools is just as important as stocking it with the right ingredients. The following are a few tools that will make your journey into Mediterranean cooking both enjoyable and efficient.

A Good Knife

A sharp, well-balanced chef's knife can make your cooking process smoother and more enjoyable. It's the most essential tool for cutting fresh vegetables and herbs, which are staples in almost every dish in the Mediterranean diet.

Cutting Boards

Multiple cutting boards allow for hygienic preparation, ensuring that there is one board for fresh produce and another for raw meats, should you choose to include them. Opting for wood or bamboo can add a rustic touch to your kitchen while also being gentle on knife blades.

Skillets and Saucepans

A sturdy skillet is perfect for sautéing vegetables, searing fish, or even whipping up a quick omelet with Mediterranean herbs. Similarly, having a range of saucepans on hand will help with cooking grains and legumes or simmering hearty stews.

Mortar and Pestle

For those who truly wish to embrace the Mediterranean way of cooking, a mortar and pestle enable you to crush fresh herbs and spices and blend them in a way that releases their full spectrum of aromatic flavors, unmatched by pre-ground spices.

Mixing Bowls

A set of mixing bowls in various sizes ensures you have a bowl for every need, be it marinating proteins, tossing salads, or letting dough rise if bread-making is on your menu.

With these essential tools and ingredients, your kitchen will be well-equipped to handle a variety of nutritious and invigorating Mediterranean meals that you can whip up with ease, even on a busy weeknight. This setup not only lends itself to efficiency but also encourages a closer connection to your food and the ways in which it nourishes both body and soul. In embracing these elements, you welcome not just the flavors but the very spirit of the Mediterranean into your home, creating dishes that are not only delicious but also deeply satisfying.

CHAPTER 1: MEDITERRANEAN DIET

Imagine a breezy afternoon overlooking the sapphire waters of the Mediterranean Sea, the air filled with the scent of olive groves and the sound of laughter as families gather around tables laden with colorful dishes. This idyllic scene is at the heart of the Mediterranean diet, not only a culinary tradition but a lifestyle embraced for centuries by people of the coastal regions from Italy to Greece. The Mediterranean diet began as a natural product of the cultural mosaic of ancient civilizations whose farming and culinary practices were deeply intertwined with their land and climate. The mild winters and hot, dry summers encouraged the growth of a rich variety of foods that are staples of the diet today olive oil, fresh fruits and vegetables, seafood, and a diverse range of grains and legumes. Coupled with this, the tradition of sharing meals and emphasizing family and community well-being crafted a blueprint for what many now recognize as one of the healthiest ways to live.

The fundamentals of the Mediterranean diet are simplistic yet profound. It advocates primarily for plant-based meals, complemented by moderate consumption of fish and poultry and an occasional indulgence in red meat. What amplifies this diet's appeal is the inclusion of daily servings of olive oil, known for its heart-healthy fats, and the permission to enjoy a glass of red wine regularly, amid family and laughter, promoting not only physical health but mental well-being.

Drawn from the idea that food should be both nourishing and a source of joy, the Mediterranean diet aligns perfectly with today's health-conscious movements while still celebrating rich, flavorful meals that can be prepared with ease. What sets it apart is not rigid calorie counting or restrictive guidelines, but a holistic approach to choosing fresh, local ingredients that naturally lead to improved health outcomes. Studies underscore its benefits, linking it to a lower risk of heart disease, metabolic syndrome, diabetes, certain cancers, depression, and Alzheimer's, particularly when combined with active living and healthy eating habits.

As we delve deeper into the chapters of this book, remember that adopting the Mediterranean diet is less about following strict rules and more about embracing a full, vibrant pattern of eating, savoring every bite, nurturing the body and soul, and fostering a love for shared meals. Let's journey together through this exploration of simple yet profound eating philosophy. Treat this not just as a diet, but as an invitation to live a longer, healthier life.

1.1 HISTORY AND ORIGINS

The sun-drenched shores of the Mediterranean basin, where the sea laps against the diverse landscapes of Europe, Africa, and Asia, are where one of the world's most admired diets originated. This diet, deeply rooted in a rich historical tapestry, is less about strict eating patterns and more about a way of living that has evolved over centuries. The Mediterranean diet, with its myriad of health benefits, is a living heritage passed down through generations of families who thrived along the Mediterranean coast.

The Cradle of Civilization

The history of the Mediterranean diet begins with the civilizations that flourished in the fertile crescent. Ancient Greece, with its philosophical sagas and epicurean delights, is often hailed as the progenitor of this diet. The Greeks emphasized dietary patterns that include fresh produce, grains, and olive oil. Later, the Romans adopted and adapted these practices, spreading them throughout the empire. The Roman influence integrated a culinary structure that emphasized balanced meals with ingredients like wheat, grapes, and olives, staples that are still predominant in the diet today.

Cultural Confluence

The historical development of the Mediterranean diet is not the story of a single region but rather a mosaic of cultural interchanges. Through conquests, trade, and migration, the diverse culinary practices of the Phoenicians, Byzantines, Moors, and Ottomans interwove with local traditions. This blend shaped a unique dietary culture characterized by a rich diversity of ingredients and flavors that is signature to the Mediterranean diet today.

Agricultural Bounty

The region's agriculture has always been propelled by its climate mild, wet winters and hot, dry summers provided ideal conditions for growing a multitude of crops. Olive trees, with their deep roots and hardy nature, flourished and became a cornerstone of the diet, both for culinary and ceremonial uses. Grapes, too, thrived under the Mediterranean sun, giving rise to a robust wine culture that is integral to the diet's emphasis on moderate consumption of red wine.

The terraced landscapes of the Mediterranean also promoted the cultivation of legumes, fruits, vegetables, and grains. These foods formed the diet's foundation, promoting health through meals centered around plant-based foods supplemented with minimal animal protein a practice modern nutritionists laud for its balance and health benefits.

Influence of Religion and Trade

Religious practices also deeply influenced the development of the Mediterranean diet. The Islamic dietary laws introduced sophisticated spice blends and cooking techniques that emphasized frugality and wholesomeness, principles that remain in the diet to this day. Meanwhile, Christianity's dietary restrictions led to an emphasis on fish and vegetables, especially during Lent. Trade routes played a crucial role in enriching the diet. The Silk Road and the spice routes brought ingredients like rice, spices, and nuts, which were creatively incorporated into local cuisines, enhancing flavors and increasing the diet's nutritional value. This era of exchange not only diversified the diet but also solidified its status as a cultural symbol of hospitality and communal living.

The Science and Spread of a Diet

It wasn't until the mid-20th century that the Mediterranean diet captured global attention. The seminal Seven Countries Study by Ancel Keys highlighted the lower incidence of heart diseases in the Mediterranean region compared to Northern Europe and the U.S., where diets were higher in saturated fats. This epidemiological study sparked a worldwide interest, drawing scientists and food enthusiasts alike to explore the benefits of the diet.

Modern Interpretation and Practices

Today, the Mediterranean diet is celebrated not just for its historical roots but for its adaptability to modern eating habits. Health professionals across the world endorse it for preventing a range of chronic diseases and for promoting longer life expectancy. This diet encourages not only a balanced intake of macronutrients but also the use of cooking methods that preserve the integrity and nutritional value of ingredients steaming, poaching, and grilling over high heat and deep-frying.

Furthermore, the diet has influenced contemporary culinary movements, championing farm-to-table practices, sustainability, and local sourcing, which resonate with today's environmentally conscious consumers. This modern interpretation reiterates the diet's foundational belief in eating not merely to nourish the body but to celebrate life and community connections.

The Mediterranean diet transcends the simple act of eating. Each meal is a celebration of flavors and a testament to the region's history, culture, and ingenuity in using what the land offers. Its continued relevance and growing popularity worldwide signal not just a trend but a sustainable approach to health and well-being a testament to its rich past and vibrant future.

In the next pages, we will delve deeper into the components that form the fabric of this dietary practice, further exploring how ancient traditions align seamlessly with modern nutritional science continuing to influence our meals and lifestyles in profound ways.

1.2 KEY COMPONENTS OF THE MEDITERRANEAN DIET

The essence of the Mediterranean diet lies not just in its ingredients, but in the symphony of flavors, nutritional balance, and the rich traditions from which it stems. As we peel back the layers of historical significance and culinary practices, the key components that define this diet offer a blueprint for a healthful way of eating and living. Let's explore these core elements that have made the Mediterranean diet a beacon of health and wellness embraced around the globe.

The Primacy of Plant-Based Foods

At the heart of the Mediterranean diet is an abiding reliance on plant-based foods. Vegetables, fruits, nuts, seeds, legumes, and whole grains form the cornerstone of daily meals. Each meal is imbued with a variety of colors and textures ensuring both nutritional richness and sensory satisfaction. Imagine the vibrant greens of spinach and arugula, the robust reds of tomatoes and peppers, and the earthy browns of lentils and whole grains. These are not just meals; they are a canvas of nature's finest produce.

Olive Oil - The Liquid Gold

If there is one emblematic ingredient that has come to define the Mediterranean diet, it is olive oil. Known affectionately as liquid gold, this essential fat is the primary cooking medium. Unlike diets high in saturated fats, the fats in olive oil are primarily "good" monounsaturated fats. These fats contribute to heart health by reducing levels of bad cholesterol. More than just a cooking oil, it's used as a salad dressing, a dipping sauce for bread, and a drizzle over cooked vegetables or grilled fish, enhancing flavors while providing nutritional benefits.

The Role of Dairy and Eggs

In moderation, dairy products, particularly those derived from goats and sheep, play a supportive role in the Mediterranean diet. Cheeses like feta and ricotta are used to enhance the flavors of dishes subtly but are consumed in much lower quantities compared to typical Western diets. Eggs, another moderate staple, are often used in cooking, providing high-quality protein and a plethora of vitamins and minerals essential for health.

Seafood - A Staple Protein

In a striking contrast to many high-protein diets prevalent in other parts of the world, the Mediterranean diet emphasizes seafood over red meat. Fish and shellfish, rich in omega-3 fatty acids, are central to the protein intake, promoting heart and brain health. Typically, seafood is consumed several times a week, prepared in ways that maintain its nutritional integrity grilled, baked, or lightly sautéed with vegetables, herbs, and a splash of lemon.

Moderate Meat and Poultry Consumption

While the Mediterranean diet enjoys a rich array of plant-based foods and seafood, red meat and poultry hold a more modest place in daily consumption. When meat is included, it is often lean cuts, consumed infrequently, making every occurrence a treat rather than a staple. This moderation supports a lower intake of saturated fats, aligning with the diet's heart-healthy ethos.

Herbs and Spices - Nature's Flavor Enhancers

Beyond just taste, the aromatic herbs and spices of the Mediterranean play crucial roles in both the flavor profile and health aspects of the diet. Rosemary, thyme, basil, and mint are not only culinary delights but are packed with antioxidants and vitamins essential for reducing inflammation and promoting overall health. Spices such as saffron, cloves, and cinnamon add exquisite flavors to meals without the need for excess salt or fat, aligning with a diet that naturalizes low sodium intake.

Wine - A Cultural Complement

In moderation, wine, particularly red wine, is considered a beneficial component of the Mediterranean diet. Consumed with meals, a glass of red wine is believed to improve heart health due to its high antioxidant content, particularly resveratrol, which has been linked to reduced inflammation and blood clot risks. However, the key lies in moderation defined as up to one glass per day for women and two for men, always consumed with food.

Community and Lifestyle

Perhaps one of the most overlooked but vital components of the Mediterranean diet is the cultural emphasis on mealtime as a communal, relaxed event. Meals are often lengthy, shared occasions that foster conversation, laughter, and family bonds. This approach to eating enhances mental and emotional well-being, turning every meal into an event and every bite into a shared celebration.

Each of these components contributes to the holistic wellness promoted by the Mediterranean diet. More than just a way of eating, it is a philosophy that advocates balance, variety, and moderation, intertwined with lifestyle choices that emphasize physical activity and social engagements. As we continue to navigate the principles of the Mediterranean diet, it becomes clear that it offers not only a guide for better eating but a pathway to a more fulfilled, health-conscious life.

1.3 HEALTH BENEFITS AND SCIENTIFIC EVIDENCE

The allure of the Mediterranean diet transcends the boundaries of taste and tradition, offering a wealth of health benefits that have been validated through decades of scientific research. As we delve into the myriad of advantages this diet provides, it becomes clear why it is often heralded as one of the most healthful dietary regimes worldwide. The Mediterranean diet isn't just food on a plate; it's preventive medicine that pleases the palate.

Cardiovascular Health

The foundational benefit of the Mediterranean diet is its impact on heart health. Rich in olive oil, nuts, and fish, which are sources of healthy monounsaturated and omega-3 fats, it naturally reduces the levels of LDL cholesterol that contribute to the clogging of arteries. The emphasis on whole grains, fruits, and vegetables also means a higher intake of fiber, which further helps to reduce blood cholesterol levels and improve vascular function.

Scientific research substantiates these claims, showcasing the diet's role in significantly reducing the risk of cardiovascular disease. Studies like the PREDIMED trial, a landmark study published in the New England Journal of Medicine, demonstrated a 30% reduction in heart attacks and stroke in high-risk individuals who adhered to a Mediterranean diet supplemented with extra-virgin olive oil or nuts. It's a compelling argument for embracing olives and whole grains over processed foods and fatty meats.

Metabolic Syndrome and Type 2 Diabetes

Beyond heart health, the Mediterranean diet also offers protective benefits against metabolic syndrome and type 2 diabetes conditions that are increasingly common due to rising rates of obesity. The diet's balance of lean proteins, low-glycemic-index fruits and vegetables, and healthy fats helps to regulate blood sugar and improve insulin sensitivity. This is crucial in a society where sugar-laden, high-carbohydrate diets are the norm.

Cognitive Benefits and Mental Health

Perhaps one of the most promising areas of research concerning the Mediterranean diet is its potential to protect cognitive function and improve mental health. Dietary patterns rich in antioxidants and anti-inflammatory components, such as the Mediterranean diet, are linked to lower levels of oxidative stress and inflammation, both of which are risk factors for cognitive decline and dementia.

Research suggests a correlation between adherence to the Mediterranean diet and a slower rate of cognitive decline. Additionally, the diet's association with reduced depression is gaining attention, possibly due to the high intake of omega-3 fatty acids, which are known to influence neurotransmitter pathways in the brain.

Longevity and Overall Mortality

Living longer, and importantly, living well, is a pivotal aspect of the Mediterranean diet's appeal. Studies consistently highlight the diet's association with increased longevity. By reducing the risk factors for chronic diseases, the diet naturally extends life expectancy. The Mediterranean diet's rich array of antioxidants, healthy fats, and fibers fights against the primary assailants that threaten longevity, including heart disease, cancer, and systemic inflammation.

Cancer Prevention

The fight against cancer finds a powerful ally in the Mediterranean diet, thanks to its emphasis on fruits and vegetables, which are loaded with essential nutrients and antioxidants. These components scavenge harmful free radicals from the body, reducing oxidative stress a leading contributor to cancer development.

Digestive Health

The Mediterranean diet benefits digestive health due to its high fiber content, which promotes regular bowel movements and the health of the gut microbiome. A diverse and balanced gut flora is crucial for digestion, absorption of nutrients, and the functioning of the immune system.

A Sustainable Approach to Weight Management

Weight management is a significant concern for many, and here again, the Mediterranean diet offers a sustainable option. Unlike diets that involve strict calorie counting or restrictive food lists, the Mediterranean diet encourages a balanced approach to eating focusing on portion control, food quality, and diversity. This encourages adherence and makes maintaining a healthy weight a more enjoyable and attainable goal.

Bridging Nutrition and Enjoyment

One of the unique aspects of the Mediterranean diet is its coupling of nutrition with pleasure. Eating is seen not just as a necessity but as an event to be enjoyed, a practice that supports psychological well-being and mindful eating. The diet's emphasis on flavor using herbs, spices, and seasonings ensures that eating healthily does not come at the expense of enjoying food.

Embracing the Mediterranean diet involves more than just changing what's on your plate; it's about altering your perspective on food. Food becomes a source of joy, a path to healing, and a way to connect with others all woven together with the thread of scientific substantiation supporting its numerous health benefits.

As we continue to explore this enriching dietary path, let it be with the knowledge that each component of the Mediterranean diet is backed by sound scientific evidence, promising not only a healthier life but a richer, more flavorful existence. It's not merely a diet but a lifestyle choice that honors both the body and the palate.

1.4 TRADITIONAL VS. MODERN MEDITERRANEAN CUISINE

As we traverse through the scenic landscapes and rich histories of the Mediterranean, the evolution of its cuisine from traditional practices to modern adaptations stands out, adapting over centuries while maintaining its essence. The Mediterranean diet, deeply rooted in ancient cultures, has not only survived but thrived, evolving seamlessly to meet modern dietary needs without losing its identity.

The Foundation of Traditional Mediterranean Cuisine

Traditional Mediterranean cuisine is the product of the geographical, cultural, and historical confluence of the region. Its cornerstone is the trio of olives, wheat, and grapes, staples that date back to ancient civilizations. These were complemented by regional herbs, fruits, vegetables, and the abundant seafood from the Mediterranean Sea, reflecting the natural resources available.

Meals were fundamentally seasonal, relying on local produce and the cycles of nature, which ensured that food was consumed in its most natural and nutritious state. This adherence to nature's rhythm also fostered a deep connection between the people, the land, and the food they consumed.

Communal Cooking and Eating

Traditionally, Mediterranean cooking was less about precise recipes and more about instinct and experience handed down through generations. Cooking was a communal activity, often centered around a communal bread oven in a village or shared meals during festivals and holidays. These practices reinforced the social fabric of the communities, making food an affair of collective participation and enjoyment.

Transition to Modern Mediterranean Cuisine

Shifts in lifestyle, globalization, and technological advancements have ushered Mediterranean cuisine into the modern age. Today, while traditional ingredients remain central, there are noticeable shifts in how food is prepared and consumed. Urban living has led to quicker meal preparations and a greater reliance on convenient, processed foods, even among Mediterranean communities.

However, unlike many dietary trends globally, modern Mediterranean cuisine has not lost its essence. It still emphasizes fresh ingredients, albeit more accessible due to improved transportation and refrigeration. The diet now includes a wider variety of foods due to global trade, incorporating ingredients like avocados and quinoa, which, while not traditional, complement the diet's principles.

Health in Tradition and Modern Adaptation

One of the most striking aspects of modern Mediterranean cuisine is its fusion with contemporary nutritional science. Today's Mediterranean recipes might incorporate less red meat and more plant-based substitutions than traditional versions due to a growing awareness of cardiovascular health and ethical concerns about meat consumption. The essence of the diet's health benefits remains preserved, adapting to new knowledge and technologies that continue to evolve dietary practices.

Influence of the Digital Age

In the digital age, the awareness and popularity of the Mediterranean diet have grown exponentially. People from non-Mediterranean regions adopt and adapt its practices, influenced by a wealth of online information, cooking shows, and health blogs. This has led to a form of globalization of the Mediterranean diet, maintaining its core principles but adapting its techniques and ingredients to local tastes and modern conveniences.

Environmental Impact and Sustainability

Modern concerns about sustainability and the environment also intersect significantly with the evolution of the Mediterranean diet. Traditional practices inherently supported sustainable agriculture through crop rotations, limited use of animal grazing, and fishing practices that did not deplete marine resources. Modern advocates of the diet emphasize these sustainable practices, highlighting the diet's low environmental impact compared to diets high in meat and processed foods.

Challenges and Opportunities

Despite its many benefits, the modern adaptation of the Mediterranean diet faces challenges. Economic factors can limit accessibility to fresh, organic produce, especially in urban settings. Moreover, lifestyle changes reducing mealtime and increasing fast food consumption challenge the diet's communal and leisurely meal traditions.

However, these challenges also present opportunities for innovation. Modern culinary initiatives are increasingly finding ways to merge traditional Mediterranean ingredients with fast, simple preparations suitable for busy lifestyles. Community gardens, farm-to-table restaurants, and local farmers' markets are reviving an interest in traditional agriculture and sustainable eating.

Cultural Preservation and Education

Ultimately, preserving the essence of Mediterranean cuisine requires a commitment not only to maintain the tradition but also to educate new generations. This includes not just recipes but the lifestyle, values, and community focus that are at the heart of the Mediterranean way of life. Through cooking classes, cultural festivals, and family meal practices, the rich tradition of Mediterranean eating continues to be passed down, maintaining its relevance in a rapidly changing world.

As we look toward the future of the Mediterranean diet, it's clear that its principles are timeless. Its ability to adapt while retaining its focus on health, community, and sustainability ensures that it will continue to be embraced by people seeking not just nourishment but a joyful, wholesome way of life. The Mediterranean diet thus stands as a bridge between the past and the future, between tradition and modernity, offering lessons in how diets can nourish us on more levels than just the physical.

1.5 INCORPORATING MEDITERRANEAN EATING INTO YOUR LIFE

Embracing the Mediterranean diet is akin to embarking on a journey that promises not just a culinary transformation but a holistic enhancement of lifestyle. Introducing the elements of Mediterranean eating into your life is not merely about changing your diet; it's about embracing a philosophy that celebrates food as a source of nourishment, joy, and togetherness. Here we explore practical ways to integrate this healthful and enriching diet into the fabric of daily life, ensuring that each meal enriches both body and soul.

Start with the Pantry

Incorporating the Mediterranean diet begins in the heart of every home the kitchen. Transforming your pantry can be a delightful adventure, stocking up on essentials like extra virgin olive oil, a variety of whole grains such as farro, bulgur, and barley, and an array of spices that will bring your dishes to life. Beans, nuts, seeds, and canned tomatoes should also have their place alongside jars of olives and capers. These staples not only inspire a multitude of dishes but also ensure that the foundation of your meals is solidly Mediterranean.

Reimagine Protein

Rethinking your protein sources is a fundamental step. While meats are enjoyed on occasion in the Mediterranean diet, the focus shifts towards plant-based proteins and seafood. Incorporating more servings of legumes, such as lentils, chickpeas, and beans, into your meals contributes to your protein intake and increases your fiber consumption. Seafood, enjoyed a couple of times a week, is prepared simply grilled, baked, or sautéed with a splash of olive oil and lemon.

Vegetables at the Center

In the Mediterranean diet, vegetables are not just a side dish; they are the centerpiece of the plate. Try to include a variety of colors and types in your meals, aiming for at least two to three servings per meal. From vibrant salads and hearty stews to grilled vegetables and satisfying purees, the options to incorporate vegetables are limitless. The key is variety and seasonality, ensuring that you enjoy the freshest produce with maximum flavor and nutritional benefits.

Healthy Fats as a Cornerstone

Replacing butter and other saturated fats with healthier fats is a cornerstone of the Mediterranean lifestyle. Olive oil is paramount, used not only for cooking but as a finishing oil drizzled over salads, soups, and bread. Nuts and seeds also play a crucial role, perfect for snacking or adding a crunchy texture to dishes, while avocados provide a creamy consistency for dressings and spreads.

Embrace Herbs and Spices

Flavoring your dishes with herbs and spices is another hallmark of Mediterranean cooking. Rather than relying on salt, seek out the herbs and spices that are prevalent in Mediterranean recipes basil, oregano, rosemary, cumin, coriander, and mint. These not only add depth and complexity to your food but also bring health benefits, including anti-inflammatory properties.

The Art of Eating

How you eat is just as important as what you eat. In Mediterranean cultures, meals are a time for relaxation and social interaction. Try to make meals a stress-free time to connect with family and friends. This practice not only enhances your mental and emotional well-being but may help improve your digestive health and metabolic profiles as you take the time to savor and digest your food thoroughly.

Integrating Seafood and Moderate Wine Consumption

For seafood lovers, adopting the Mediterranean way offers a splendid array of options. Fish such as salmon, mackerel, and sardines are not only delicious but are excellent sources of omega-3 fatty acids. When it comes to alcohol, moderation is key; if you already consume alcohol, the Mediterranean diet considers a glass of red wine during meals as beneficial due to its antioxidants.

Sweets in Moderation

Sweets are not an everyday treat in the Mediterranean diet. When desserts are consumed, they are often fruit-based and use natural sweeteners like honey, incorporating healthful nuts and citrus. This approach allows you to enjoy the occasional sweet treat without compromising health.

Stay Active

The Mediterranean lifestyle is not just about diet but also includes regular physical activity. Integrating daily activities like walking, gardening, or yoga can complement your diet changes and enhance the benefits of Mediterranean eating.

Continuous Learning and Experimentation

Embracing the Mediterranean diet is a continuous journey of learning and experimentation. Each meal is an opportunity to explore new flavors and dishes while making incremental changes that collectively transform your eating habits. Cooking Mediterranean meals can become a joyful exploration, connecting you with a rich culinary tradition that emphasizes health, simplicity, and community.

By incorporating these elements into your life, the Mediterranean diet transcends from being just a way of eating to becoming a sustainable lifestyle, promoting not only longevity but a greater quality of life. Living the Mediterranean way is about finding joy in every meal and sharing that joy with loved ones, a truly nourishing experience that feeds both the body and the soul.

Chapter 2: Only 5 Ingredients

In the bustling rhythm of our daily lives, the call to simplicity feels almost revolutionary. Enter the world of 5-ingredient cooking a space where simplicity melds beautifully with the rich flavors and wholesome nutrition of the Mediterranean diet. This charming approach is not just a trend, but a timeless philosophy that underpins some of the most delightful and easy-to-make dishes you can imagine.

When we pare down our ingredient lists, each component shines brightly, bringing its unique character to the meal without the noise of unnecessary extras. The Mediterranean diet, celebrated for its health benefits and sensory pleasures, aligns perfectly with this minimalist cooking style. It highlights the natural flavors of fresh produce, heart-healthy fats, and protein-rich legumes and seafood, transforming them into stunning meals with no need for complexity.

Imagine you are walking through a vibrant Mediterranean market. You pick up some ripe tomatoes, a few fresh basil leaves, a block of feta cheese, olives, and a loaf of crusty bread. With just these five ingredients, you have the makings of a delightful bruschetta that brings a taste of coastal Italy right to your table. This is the essence of 5-ingredient cooking simple ingredients coming together to create magic.

In this chapter, we delve into how you can maximize flavors with fewer ingredients, ensuring that every meal is both a nourishing and fulfilling experience. The strategies discussed here aren't just about cutting down your shopping list but are rooted in the cherished culinary traditions of Mediterranean cultures. They have mastered the art of doing more with less, a lesson very much needed in our 'more is better' world.

As you journey through the following pages, remember that each meal you prepare is an act of love for yourself, your body, and those you share your table with. Let's embrace the simplicity, the healthfulness, and the joy that 5-ingredient meals bring into our hectic lives. Here's to finding beauty in simplicity and to making every ingredient count!

2.1 THE PHILOSOPHY BEHIND 5-INGREDIENT COOKING

In the heart of every culinary tradition lies a philosophy, a guiding principle that shapes the approach to cooking and eating. For the Mediterranean peoples, this has always been about simplicity and respect for good, local ingredients. Our modern kitchens, inundated with gadgets and complex recipes, can sometimes lose sight of this foundational truth. But therein lies the charm and opportunity of 5-ingredient cooking it reminds us of the value in simplicity and offers a practical methodology that aligns beautifully with our lives today.

Understanding the philosophy behind 5-ingredient cooking starts with an appreciation for the ingredients themselves. In a world where food can be heavily processed and recipes overly complicated, choosing to cook with only five ingredients is an homage to the essence of each component. This method not only enhances the natural flavors but also ensures that the nutrients are retained, leading to healthier, more wholesome meals.

The limited number of ingredients compels us to prioritize quality over quantity. It encourages us to shop locally, selecting the freshest and finest items our community has to offer ripe, succulent tomatoes; aromatic, freshly-picked basil; cold-pressed olive oil rich in flavor and heart-healthy fats. This selective shopping practice showcases the Mediterranean's season-based eating ethos, where meals reflect the rhythms of nature and celebrate the produce at its peak.

But the philosophy runs deeper than the ingredients it's also about embedding mindfulness into our daily routines. With fewer ingredients to handle and steps to follow, cooking no longer feels like just another task amidst our hectic schedules. Instead, it becomes a pleasurable activity, a moment to decelerate and engage fully with what we are doing. This slower pace allows us to appreciate the sensory joys of cooking: the vibrant colors of vegetables, the sizzle of olive oil in the pan, the fragrant release of herbs. Each action is intentional, each addition thoughtfully considered, transforming cooking from routine to ritual.

Moreover, this approach invites innovation. When we limit our ingredients, we're pushed to think creatively about how to maximize their impact. How can a drizzle of balsamic vinegar bring alive a dish's flavors, or a pinch of sea salt heighten the sweetness in a slice of melon? This kind of thinking reconnects us with the intuitive skills of traditional cooks who could craft extraordinary dishes with the most ordinary of ingredients.

In simplifying our approach, we also address many of the modern world's concerns around food sustainability, health, and time efficiency. Cooking with fewer ingredients naturally cuts down on food waste, as we're more likely to use up the entirety of what we buy. It makes meals easier to prepare, ideal for busy individuals who still wish to enjoy a homemade dinner without spending hours in the kitchen. And, of course, choosing unprocessed, fresh, natural ingredients supports a healthier lifestyle, echoing the well-documented benefits of the Mediterranean diet on longevity and wellbeing.

The enchantment of 5-ingredient cooking doesn't stop at what it does for our physical health and our pace of life; it also fosters social connections. Meals inspired by this approach tend to be straightforward, removing the intimidation factor of presenting a multi-course, elaborate dinner. This simplicity encourages us to cook with others, including family members who might otherwise feel sidelined by the complexity of traditional recipes. It promotes gathering around the table, sharing the joys of a meal created together even if it's just a weekday dinner.

Importantly, 5-ingredient cooking aligns with the resourcefulness ingrained in Mediterranean cultures, where nothing goes to waste and everything has value. This philosophy instills a sense of gratitude and respect for the food on our plates, inspired by generations of cooks who made do with what they had, often under constraints far tighter than ours. It's a lesson in culinary creativity as much as it is in humility and sustainability.

Ultimately, the philosophy behind 5-ingredient cooking is about returning to basics and reassessing what is truly necessary for nourishment both bodily and spiritually. It champions a diet that is as good for the mind as it is for the body, infused with the goodness of simple food prepared in a simple way. This approach doesn't just change how we cook; it transforms how we think about food, how we consume it, and how we share it. It rekindles an old-world wisdom that we, amidst our fast-paced and often disconnected lives, are in dire need of remembering.

In embracing the minimalist ethos of 5-ingredient cooking, we rediscover the joy of preparing meals that are as nourishing to prepare as they are to eat. We engage in a practice that encourages us to slow down, savor the moment, and connect be it with food, with nature, or with each other. Such is the transformative power of a philosophy rooted deeply in one of the world's healthiest and most sustainable diets.

2.2 PANTRY ESSENTIALS FOR QUICK MEALS

Embodying the philosophy of 5-ingredient cooking begins with a well-thought-out pantry. This foundation establishes not only your ability to pull together quick, delightful meals but also connects you to the greater Mediterranean tradition of using high-quality, staple ingredients to produce timelessly delicious and deeply nourishing dishes. The pantry of a 5-ingredient chef is more than just a storage space it's the heart of every meal, enabling creativity and ensuring that even your simplest dishes are vibrant and satisfying.

First, consider the essential nature of oils in Mediterranean cooking. The king of these, undoubtedly, is extra-virgin olive oil, known for its rich flavor and health benefits, particularly its heart-healthy fats. Having a bottle of high-quality olive oil at your disposal means you're ready to add depth and character to any dish, whether drizzling it generously over salad greens, using it as a base for sauces, or simply using it to sauté vegetables.

Next, no Mediterranean pantry is complete without a variety of vinegars. Balsamic vinegar, with its sweet and tangy profile, can enhance the natural sweetness of roasted vegetables and salads. Red and white wine vinegars are perfect for sharper, brighter vinaigrettes or to deglaze a pan to make a simple yet flavorful sauce.

Herbs and spices are the soul of Mediterranean cooking, bringing dishes to life with minimal effort. Keeping dried oregano, thyme, rosemary, and basil on hand allows for versatility in flavor. Similarly, sea salt and freshly ground black pepper are essential for enhancing natural flavors without overshadowing the primary ingredients. Using herbs and spices effectively means that you can always ensure your meals are lively and memorable, even when they are astoundingly simple.

For those preferring grains, whole grains like farro, barley, and quinoa not only hold a place in the traditional Mediterranean pantry but are also power-packed with nutrients. They can serve as the base for a plethora of dishes, from salads to side dishes, absorbing flavors beautifully while offering satisfying textures that complement both vegetable and meat dishes.

Legumes, such as lentils, chickpeas, and beans, are staples for adding body and protein to your meals. They are particularly wonderful in the Mediterranean diet as they can be transformed into soups, salads, or even blended into dips. Having canned versions on hand can be a convenient and quick way to incorporate them into meals, especially when time doesn't allow for soaking and cooking dried legumes.

Canned tomatoes are another powerhouse in the kitchen. They can form the base of sauces, lend acidity and richness to stews, or simply be used to throw together a quick, rustic soup. The versatility and intensified flavor of quality canned tomatoes can rescue even the most hurried of meal preparations.

Turning to nuts and seeds, ingredients like almonds, pine nuts, or sunflower seeds offer crunch, protein, and a richness that complements the natural sweetness and profiles of many fruits and vegetables used in Mediterranean cooking. They are perfect for adding to salads, sprinkling over cooked dishes, or even incorporating into desserts.

Finally, no Mediterranean pantry is complete without the inclusion of cheeses and yogurts. A block of feta or Parmesan can dramatically elevate a dish, offering saltiness and texture that balance well with the Mediterranean palette of flavors. Greek yogurt serves a dual purpose, functioning as a creamy base for dips or a tangy, enriching addition to sauces.

Each of these components plays a crucial part in the Mediterranean culinary repertoire, particularly when embracing the 5-ingredient philosophy. These staples provide not only convenience and efficiency but also ensure that every meal, no matter how quickly it is prepared, holds true to the healthy and flavorful principles of Mediterranean eating.

Creating a strategic pantry is akin to setting a painter before an easel, equipped with the best colors for their palette. It is about anticipating your needs, understanding the versatility of each ingredient, and harnessing the potential of simple foods to create something that is much more than the sum of its parts. With these essentials, assembled with care and consideration, you are well-prepared to embark on a journey of flavorful, healthy, and straightforward cooking that brings the essence of the Mediterranean into your kitchen.

2.3 HOW TO MAXIMIZE FLAVOR WITH MINIMAL INGREDIENTS

In the symphony of cooking, the art of maximizing flavor with minimal ingredients is akin to mastering a minimalist musical score. Every note counts, every pause is significant, and every instrument, no matter how subtle, plays a crucial role in harmonizing the whole piece. In the context of the Mediterranean diet renowned for its simple yet robust flavors how do chefs and home cooks alike create memorable dishes with just a handful of ingredients? The key lies in understanding the intrinsic properties of each element and leveraging classical cooking techniques to enhance and amplify their natural flavors.

The cornerstone of this flavor-maximizing approach begins with the selection of ingredients themselves. Quality cannot be understated when your palette is limited. For instance, choosing a richly flavored extra-virgin olive oil, a ripe, sun-kissed tomato, or a fresh catch of sea bass can make the difference between a flat dish and one that sings with authenticity and depth. Much like a painter selects premium colors for their palette, so must the cook choose ingredients that offer the most potent and expressive flavors.

Once high-quality ingredients are secured, the next step is to apply heat intelligently. Cooking methods like roasting, grilling, and sautéing are favored in Mediterranean kitchens for their ability to concentrate and caramelize natural sugars within foods, thus deepening flavors. Roasting vegetables, for instance, can transform the humblest carrot or zucchini into something sweet, intense, and complex. Similarly, grilling can impart a smoky nuance to meats and vegetables, invoking the primal essence of fire-cooked meals that resonate on a sensory level.

Layering flavors is another essential tactic. Even when using few ingredients, one can achieve layers of taste by the thoughtful addition of herbs and spices at different cooking stages. For instance, adding garlic early in the cooking process imbues the oil with a mellow, sweet flavor, while introducing it at the end can give a sharp, pronounced bite. This strategic timing can dramatically alter the taste experience of a dish.

Acid, too, plays a pivotal role in the Mediterranean flavor arsenal. A squeeze of lemon, a dash of vinegar, or a spoonful of sumac can brighten dishes and lift other flavors, cutting through fat and richness to introduce a fresh dimension. This is why lemon trees and vine stocks are prolific across Mediterranean coasts, their fruits ready to enliven an array of culinary creations.

Salt is perhaps the most indispensable tool for maximizing flavor. Beyond merely seasoning food, salt can heighten other taste profiles. A pinch can reduce bitterness, balance sweetness, and turn a bland dish into a vibrant offering. It's the bridge that connects all other flavors, creating harmony on the palate.

While fresh ingredients deliver remarkable flavors, the art of simmering can also be employed to meld ingredients together, allowing them to exchange and absorb each other's essences. A simple tomato sauce, left to simmer slowly, develops a rich, integrated flavor impossible to achieve through quick cooking. Similarly, slow-cooked legumes in a stew can adopt the smoky tastes of paprika and the sharpness of onions to render a dish where every spoonful is layered with history and culture.

To further capture depth, textures play an often-underappreciated role in the maximizing of flavor. The contrast in textures can make a dish more enjoyable and give the impression of complexity from simple ingredients. Creamy with crunchy, soft alongside firm these juxtapositions engage the senses more fully, encouraging a more mindful eating experience.

Moreover, the use of fresh garnishes not only adds visual appeal but also introduces vibrant, raw flavors that can contrast beautifully with the cooked elements of a dish. A handful of fresh basil over a slow-roasted tomato soup, or some freshly grated lemon zest atop grilled fish, can elevate a dish from delicious to sublime.

Lastly, personal touches are what truly allow flavors to flourish. The individuality of a cook can shine through in the way they balance or contrast flavors. Personal intuition plays a critical role, and like any art, cooking allows one to express mood, emotion, and creativity, which are conveyed through the flavors on the plate.

By acknowledging and celebrating each ingredient's potential, integrating wise cooking methods, and playing with contrasts and complements, every cook can transform simple dishes into exceptional experiences. The philosophy of maximizing flavor with minimal ingredients isn't just about making do with less; it's about celebrating more with what you have, focusing on quality, care, and creativity to turn everyday eating into an artful way of living.

2.4 SIMPLE SUBSTITUTIONS FOR VARIETY

Embracing the philosophy of 5-ingredient cooking introduces a delightful challenge: how to vary dishes while maintaining simplicity. This endeavor cultivates creativity, encourages flexibility, and ensures our meals remain exciting and diverse. Here, the art of substitution plays a critical role, offering ways to alter flavors and textures without complicating the ingredient list.

Substitutions in cooking are akin to variations in a melody. A skilled musician can take a simple tune and, by altering a few notes, present a whole new theme that retains the essence of the original. Similarly, with a well-considered substitution, a familiar dish can be transformed into something novel and refreshing while maintaining its foundational character.

One of the most common areas for substitutions is in proteins. Depending on availability, dietary preferences, or simply to introduce variety, the protein in a dish can be swapped without altering the core concept. For instance, chicken might be the go-to choice for a quick sauté, but replacing it with shrimp, tofu, or a hearty bean can cater to different dietary needs and preferences while keeping the preparation straightforward.

Vegetables offer a playground of variety. Seasonal changes and regional availability can influence what's at hand in the kitchen, necessitating adjustments. A recipe that originally calls for zucchini can be adapted to feature bell peppers, eggplants, or asparagus depending on what's in season. This not only introduces different flavors and textures but also encourages eating locally and seasonally echoing traditional Mediterranean practices.

Dairy products in recipes also present substitution opportunities. Various types of cheese, for instance, can dramatically change a dish's profile. Swapping feta cheese in a salad for shaved Parmesan offers a different texture and a sharper taste, or using yogurt instead of cream in sauce can lighten a dish while still providing a creamy texture.

Herbs and spices are perhaps where a simple substitution can have the most immediate impact. Depending on the desired flavor profile, changing just one spice or herb can take a dish from one region of the Mediterranean to another. Substitute oregano with some saffron, and suddenly, a Greek-inspired dish takes on a Spanish flair. This versatility is especially valuable in 5-ingredient cooking, where each element's flavor impact is magnified.

Beyond just swapping one ingredient for another, there are ways to substitute techniques that can also create variety. For instance, if a recipe typically involves roasting, trying a quick pan-sear might yield a delightful change in texture and flavor, bringing out a different aspect of the ingredients. Similarly, changing how ingredients are cut or presented can alter the eating experience. A thinly sliced radish behaves differently on the palate than a chunky one, and can significantly enhance a dish's aesthetic appeal.

Sometimes, substitutions come from necessity, such as adapting recipes for allergens or dietary restrictions. Gluten-free grains like quinoa or buckwheat can replace traditional wheat products. Nut allergies can prompt the use of seeds, such as sunflower or pumpkin, which can serve a similar textural purpose in recipes. Adapting dishes to meet these needs doesn't have to feel like a compromise but rather an exploration of the diverse bounty our diets can include.

Moreover, understanding the underlying reason why an ingredient is used in a recipe can guide effective substitutions. If a recipe uses lemon for acidity, other acidic components like vinegar or even tamarind can stand in when lemon is unavailable. This deeper comprehension of cooking principles not only makes for successful substitutions but also enriches the cooking experience imbuing the cook with confidence and a richer understanding of culinary science.

It's also enlightening to experiment with pairing substitutions, considering how changing two or more ingredients in concert can harmonize differently and bring new life to a recipe. For instance substituting both the protein and the spice profile in a dish could transport its geographic flavor base from the cliffs of Santorini to the bustling markets of Marrakech.

Ultimately, smart, thoughtful substitutions in 5-ingredient cooking ensure that each meal remains fresh, exciting, and suited to the moment's specific needs. Such adaptability not only reflects the resourcefulness of traditional Mediterranean cooks but also speaks to modern cooks' creativity in our global pantry. Substitutions allow us to weave personal stories into our meals, transforming every dish into a tapestry of cultural and personal expression, all while maintaining simplicity and elegance at the table.

2.5 COOKING TECHNIQUES FOR QUICK AND HEALTHY MEALS

The secret to vibrant and healthful meals often lies not just in the ingredients used but also in how they are cooked. In 5-ingredient cooking, where simplicity reigns, leveraging certain techniques can make all the difference, enhancing flavors, preserving nutrients, and ensuring meals are prepared both swiftly and healthily. Cooking, in this context, becomes an elegant dance of temperature, time, and texture, each step carefully choreographed to yield dishes that are fulfilling yet effortless.

One of the most effective techniques in cooking for both speed and health is sautéing. Using just a small amount of quality olive oil over relatively high heat, one can quickly cook vegetables, meat, or fish, creating a dish that is tender yet crisp. The key here is to keep the food moving in the pan, allowing it to cook evenly and locking in flavor and moisture without overcooking.

Steaming stands out as another stellar cooking method, especially for preserving the integrity and nutritional quality of vegetables. This gentle technique uses the steam from boiling water to cook the food, ensuring that it retains much of its original color, texture, mineral content, and vitamins which are often lost through methods like boiling.

Grilling imbues dishes with a distinct charred flavor that is both rustic and profound. It is a technique that doesn't rely heavily on fats or oils, making it ideal for a health-conscious diet. Whether it's vegetables, seafood, or lean meats, grilling enhances the natural flavors of foods without the need for much seasoning, embracing the elemental taste that comes from fire cooking.

Another valuable technique is roasting, particularly for its capacity to intensify the natural flavors in ingredients. Roasting can transform the inherent sweetness of vegetables like bell peppers, tomatoes, and onions, or create a tender, flavorful crust on meats and fish. The process of roasting circulates heat around the food, allowing it to cook evenly and develop a delightful texture and deep flavors.

Braising is a hybrid cooking method that combines sautéing initially and then simmering in a small amount of liquid. This technique is particularly suited for tougher cuts of meat and dense vegetables. It tenderizes by breaking down fibers, melding flavors in a luxuriously slow cook that saturates the food in aromatic spice and herb-infused broths or wines.

Each of these methods showcases how heat can be harnessed to sculpt ingredients into their most pleasing forms. Yet, cooking techniques are not solely about heat application. Preparatory techniques also play a pivotal role in the creation of meals that are quick to prepare and nutritious.

For instance, the act of marinating can prepare foods for quicker cooking times while enhancing flavor. A simple marinade might include lemon juice, herbs, and oil left to mingle with the main ingredient for a few hours or overnight. This not only infuses the dish with robust flavors but also can help tenderize meats or meld the flavors more deeply in tofu or vegetables.

Similarly, the preparation of ingredients such as chopping, dicing, or julienning can influence cooking time and the dish's final presentation. Smaller, uniformly cut pieces cook more rapidly and absorb flavors more thoroughly, reducing overall kitchen time without sacrificing taste.

Moreover, understanding how to layer flavors with a minimal number of ingredients such as by toasting spices or deglazing a pan to incorporate browned bits into sauces can add dimensions of taste without additional components. These simple gestures make maximum use of each ingredient's potential, echoing the essence of Mediterranean culinary tradition, where nothing is wasted, and everything is celebrated.

Technique in cooking is like language in poetry. It is not just about what is created but how it is expressed. Understanding the how's of cooking expands the range of what can be achieved within the confines of five simple ingredients. It allows for exploration and improvisation, giving the home cook or the seasoned chef the tools needed to adapt to tastes, seasons, and what lies in the pantry without feeling constrained.

Indeed, mastering these cooking techniques ensures that every meal, no matter how quick or straightforward, carries with it a touch of culinary artistry a testament to the power of cooking to transform everyday ingredients into extraordinary experiences. Engaging with these methods can turn the simple act of preparing a meal into an opportunity for creativity and connection, elevating the everyday into something truly remarkable.

Ah, breakfast the meal that beckons us awake each morning, reigniting our senses and preparing us for the day ahead. In the Mediterranean, breakfast isn't just a hurried fuel stop; it's an intentional, joyous occasion that sets the tone for the day's unfolding stories. Through the simple mastery of five ingredients, each breakfast recipe in this chapter embodies that very essence of the Mediterranean lifestyle: freshness, simplicity, and vitality.

Imagine opening your day with a meal that reflects the warm sun, the gentle sea breeze, and the vibrant colors of the Mediterranean basin. Think of savoring a dish where every ingredient can be tasted distinctly, each bite a testament to a culture that has revered the art of eating well as a pathway to living well.

Here, we don't just throw together nondescript meals; we build traditions on our plate. Consider the classic Greek dish of tomatoes and feta, seasoned only with fine olive oil and a sprinkle of oregano it's simple, yet every mouthful is a burst of sun-kissed joy. Or perhaps a Turkish-inspired poached egg, gently laid over a bed of garlicky yogurt and drizzled with chili oil. And let's not forget about a slice of whole-grain bread, a staple in many Mediterranean homes, topped with whatever fresh, local produce you might have at hand.

Each recipe I'll share slinks away from the complex spice arsenals and lengthy preparations. Instead, we're going back to basics, empowering you to create splendid, nourishing meals even within the swirl of a hurried morning. After all, the true Mediterranean way intertwines pleasure with health, simplicity with richness, all wrapped up in the quiet joy of the morning's first hours.

As we journey through the recipes, remember: every single one is designed not just to satisfy hunger but to enrich your life, creating moments of connection, whether at a bustling family table or in the quiet contemplation of your morning ritual. Each dish tells a story, and with only five ingredients, you're invited to take part in this narrative of flavor, heritage, and health. Clear, vivid and uncomplicated welcome to your Mediterranean morning.

3.1 5-Ingredient Breakfast Ideas

GREEK YOGURT WITH HONEY AND WALNUTS

PREPARATION TIME: 5 min

COOKING TIME: 0 min

MODE OF COOKING: No-cook

SERVINGS: 2

INGREDIENTS:

- 1 cup Greek yogurt
- 2 Tbsp honey
- 1/4 cup walnuts, chopped
- 1 tsp ground cinnamon
- 1/2 cup fresh berries (optional)

DIRECTIONS:

1. Divide Greek yogurt into two serving bowls.
2. Drizzle 1 Tbsp of honey over each bowl of yogurt.
3. Sprinkle the chopped walnuts evenly over the yogurt.
4. Dust with ground cinnamon.
5. Add fresh berries on top if desired.

TIPS:

- Use local honey for a more authentic flavor.
- Swap walnuts for almonds for a different texture.

N.V.: Calories: 240, Fat: 10g, Carbs: 30g, Protein: 12g, Sugar: 24g, Sodium: 50mg, Potassium: 220mg, Cholesterol: 10mg

AVOCADO AND EGG TOAST

PREPARATION TIME: 5 min

COOKING TIME: 5 min

MODE OF COOKING: Toasting and frying

SERVINGS: 2

INGREDIENTS:

- 2 slices whole grain bread
- 1 ripe avocado
- 2 eggs
- 1 Tbsp olive oil
- Salt and pepper to taste

DIRECTIONS:

1. Toast the bread slices to desired crispness.
2. While the bread is toasting, heat olive oil in a small skillet over medium heat.
3. Fry the eggs until the whites are set but the yolks are still runny.

4. Mash the avocado and spread it evenly on the toasted bread.

5. Place a fried egg on top of each slice of avocado toast.

6. Season with salt and pepper to taste.

TIPS:

- Add a sprinkle of red pepper flakes for a spicy kick.

- Use a ripe, creamy avocado for the best texture.

N.V.: Calories: 300, Fat: 22g, Carbs: 22g, Protein: 10g, Sugar: 2g, Sodium: 240mg, Potassium: 580mg, Cholesterol: 185mg

TOMATO AND FETA CHEESE OMELET

PREPARATION TIME: 5 min

COOKING TIME: 10 min

MODE OF COOKING: Frying

SERVINGS: 2

INGREDIENTS:

- 4 eggs
- 1/2 cup cherry tomatoes, halved
- 1/4 cup feta cheese, crumbled
- 1 Tbsp olive oil
- Fresh basil leaves, chopped

DIRECTIONS:

1. Whisk the eggs in a bowl until well combined.

2. Heat olive oil in a non-stick skillet over medium heat.

3. Pour the eggs into the skillet and cook until they begin to set.

4. Add the cherry tomatoes and feta cheese on one half of the omelet.

5. Fold the omelet in half and cook until the cheese is slightly melted.

6. Sprinkle with fresh basil before serving.

TIPS:

- Serve with a side of whole-grain toast for a complete meal.

- Use heirloom tomatoes for extra flavor.

N.V.: Calories: 250, Fat: 20g, Carbs: 5g, Protein: 14g, Sugar: 2g, Sodium: 300mg, Potassium: 350mg, Cholesterol: 375mg

MEDITERRANEAN SMOOTHIE BOWL

PREPARATION TIME: 10 min

COOKING TIME: 0 min

MODE OF COOKING: Blending

SERVINGS: 2

INGREDIENTS:

- 1 cup Greek yogurt
- 1 banana
- 1/2 cup fresh strawberries
- 1/4 cup almonds, sliced
- 1 Tbsp honey

DIRECTIONS:

1. Blend Greek yogurt, banana, and strawberries until smooth.

2. Pour the smoothie into two bowls.

3. Top with sliced almonds and a drizzle of honey.

TIPS:

- Add a handful of spinach for extra nutrients without altering the taste.

- Use frozen fruit for a thicker consistency.

N.V.: Calories: 290, Fat: 12g, Carbs: 38g, Protein: 12g, Sugar: 24g, Sodium: 50mg, Potassium: 470mg, Cholesterol: 5mg

SPINACH AND FETA STUFFED PEPPERS

PREPARATION TIME: 10 min

COOKING TIME: 15 min

MODE OF COOKING: Baking

SERVINGS: 2

INGREDIENTS:

- 2 bell peppers, halved and seeded
- 1 cup fresh spinach, chopped
- 1/4 cup feta cheese, crumbled
- 2 Tbsp olive oil
- Salt and pepper to taste

DIRECTIONS:

1. Preheat oven to 375°F (190°C).
2. Drizzle olive oil over the bell pepper halves.
3. Stuff each pepper with chopped spinach and sprinkle with feta cheese.
4. Place stuffed peppers on a baking sheet and bake for 15 minutes or until peppers are tender.
5. Season with salt and pepper before serving.

TIPS:

- Use a mix of red and yellow peppers for a colorful presentation.
- Add a squeeze of lemon juice for extra freshness.

N.V.: Calories: 200, Fat: 15g, Carbs: 10g, Protein: 5g, Sugar: 5g, Sodium: 300mg, Potassium: 400mg, Cholesterol: 15mg

BANANA AND ALMOND BUTTER TOAST

PREPARATION TIME: 5 min

COOKING TIME: 0 min

MODE OF COOKING: No-cook

SERVINGS: 2

INGREDIENTS:

- 2 slices whole grain bread
- 2 Tbsp almond butter
- 1 banana, sliced
- 1 Tbsp honey
- 1 tsp chia seeds

DIRECTIONS:

1. Toast the bread slices to desired crispness.
2. Spread almond butter evenly on each slice of toast.
3. Top with banana slices.
4. Drizzle with honey and sprinkle chia seeds on top.

TIPS:

- Use crunchy almond butter for added texture.
- Substitute honey with maple syrup for a different flavor profile.

N.V.: Calories: 320, Fat: 15g, Carbs: 38g, Protein: 8g, Sugar: 18g, Sodium: 150mg, Potassium: 450mg, Cholesterol: 0mg

MEDITERRANEAN BREAKFAST BURRITO

PREPARATION TIME: 10 min

COOKING TIME: 5 min

MODE OF COOKING: Frying

SERVINGS: 2

INGREDIENTS:

- 4 eggs
- 1/2 cup diced tomatoes
- 1/4 cup feta cheese, crumbled
- 2 whole wheat tortillas
- 1 Tbsp olive oil

DIRECTIONS:

1. Whisk the eggs in a bowl until well combined.
2. Heat olive oil in a non-stick skillet over medium heat.
3. Add the eggs and cook, stirring, until scrambled.
4. Divide the scrambled eggs between the two tortillas.
5. Top with diced tomatoes and crumbled feta cheese.
6. Roll up the tortillas to form burritos.

TIPS:

- Serve with a side of fresh salsa for extra flavor.
- Add spinach for an extra nutrient boost.

N.V.: Calories: 350, Fat: 20g, Carbs: 25g, Protein: 18g, Sugar: 4g, Sodium: 450mg, Potassium: 350mg, Cholesterol: 380mg

SMOKED SALMON AND AVOCADO TOAST

PREPARATION TIME: 5 min

COOKING TIME: 0 min

MODE OF COOKING: No-cook

SERVINGS: 2

INGREDIENTS:

- 2 slices whole grain bread
- 1 ripe avocado
- 2 oz smoked salmon
- 1 Tbsp lemon juice
- Salt and pepper to taste

DIRECTIONS:

1. Toast the bread slices to desired crispness.
2. Mash the avocado with lemon juice, salt, and pepper.
3. Spread the avocado mixture on the toasted bread.
4. Top with smoked salmon.

TIPS:

- Garnish with capers for added flavor.
- Use a sprinkle of dill for a fresh, herby taste.

N.V.: Calories: 280, Fat: 18g, Carbs: 20g, Protein: 12g, Sugar: 2g, Sodium: 350mg, Potassium: 450mg, Cholesterol: 20mg

MEDITERRANEAN QUINOA BREAKFAST BOWL

PREPARATION TIME: 5 min

COOKING TIME: 15 min

MODE OF COOKING: Boiling

SERVINGS: 2

INGREDIENTS:

- 1 cup cooked quinoa
- 1/2 cup cherry tomatoes, halved
- 1/4 cup kalamata olives, sliced
- 1/4 cup feta cheese, crumbled
- 2 Tbsp olive oil

DIRECTIONS:

1. Cook quinoa according to package instructions and let cool slightly.
2. Divide the quinoa into two bowls.
3. Top with cherry tomatoes, kalamata olives, and feta cheese.
4. Drizzle with olive oil.

TIPS:

- Add a squeeze of lemon juice for a fresh, tangy flavor.
- Use pre-cooked quinoa to save time.

N.V.: Calories: 350, Fat: 18g, Carbs: 32g, Protein: 12g, Sugar: 3g, Sodium: 400mg, Potassium: 450mg, Cholesterol: 15mg

RICOTTA AND HONEY TOAST

PREPARATION TIME: 5 min

COOKING TIME: 0 min

MODE OF COOKING: No-cook

SERVINGS: 2

INGREDIENTS:

- 2 slices whole grain bread
- 1/2 cup ricotta cheese
- 2 Tbsp honey
- 1 tsp lemon zest
- Fresh mint leaves for garnish

DIRECTIONS:

1. Toast the bread slices to desired crispness.
2. Spread ricotta cheese evenly on each slice of toast.
3. Drizzle with honey.
4. Sprinkle with lemon zest.
5. Garnish with fresh mint leaves.

TIPS:

- Use local honey for a more authentic flavor.
- Substitute ricotta with Greek yogurt for a different taste.

N.V.: Calories: 320, Fat: 12g, Carbs: 38g, Protein: 12g, Sugar: 18g, Sodium: 150mg, Potassium: 250mg, Cholesterol: 20mg

MEDITERRANEAN EGG MUFFINS

PREPARATION TIME: 10 min

COOKING TIME: 20 min

MODE OF COOKING: Baking

SERVINGS: 6

INGREDIENTS:

- 6 eggs
- 1/2 cup spinach, chopped
- 1/4 cup sun-dried tomatoes, chopped
- 1/4 cup feta cheese, crumbled
- 1 Tbsp olive oil

DIRECTIONS:

1. Preheat oven to 350°F (175°C).
2. Grease a muffin tin with olive oil.
3. Whisk the eggs in a bowl.
4. Add spinach, sun-dried tomatoes, and feta cheese to the eggs.
5. Pour the egg mixture into the muffin tin.
6. Bake for 20 minutes or until the muffins are set.

TIPS:

- Make a batch ahead of time and store in the fridge for quick breakfasts.
- Use silicone muffin liners for easy removal.

N.V.: Calories: 100, Fat: 7g, Carbs: 2g, Protein: 7g, Sugar: 1g, Sodium: 200mg, Potassium: 100mg, Cholesterol: 150mg

MEDITERRANEAN BREAKFAST SALAD

PREPARATION TIME: 10 min

COOKING TIME: 0 min

MODE OF COOKING: No-cook

SERVINGS: 2

INGREDIENTS:

- 2 cups mixed greens
- 1/2 cup cherry tomatoes, halved
- 1/4 cup cucumber, sliced
- 1/4 cup feta cheese, crumbled
- 2 Tbsp olive oil

DIRECTIONS:

1. Divide the mixed greens between two plates.
2. Top with cherry tomatoes, cucumber, and feta cheese.
3. Drizzle with olive oil.

TIPS:

- Add a poached egg on top for extra protein.
- Sprinkle with oregano for added flavor.

N.V.: Calories: 200, Fat: 16g, Carbs: 8g, Protein: 6g, Sugar: 4g, Sodium: 250mg, Potassium: 350mg, Cholesterol: 15mg

Imagine a breezy, sunlit afternoon along the Mediterranean coast, where the simple pleasure of a fresh, flavorful salad or a hearty bowl of soup embodies the essence of local eating habits. In this chapter, we dive into the heart of simplicity with recipes that spotlight the vibrant, robust flavors of the Mediterranean diet, using no more than five essential ingredients.

Soups and salads, in many cultures, are just side dishes or starters, but in the Mediterranean, they often take center stage. Each bowl and plate is a testament to the region's bountiful produce and the age-old wisdom of making much with little. With a few staple ingredients like ripe tomatoes, crisp cucumbers, extra virgin olive oil, and fresh herbs, one can concoct a dish that is both nourishing and delightfully satisfying.

The beauty of these recipes lies in their simplicity and adaptability. Whether it's a chilly evening needing the warmth of a lentil soup or a hot summer day perfect for a cool, crisp Greek salad, the principles of Mediterranean cooking remain the same: fresh ingredients, simple techniques, and a focus on enhancing natural flavors rather than masking them.

So why soups and salads? They are the perfect canvas to demonstrate how a minimalistic approach to ingredients can lead to maximum flavor. Each recipe in this chapter adheres to easy preparations and quick cooking methods, ensuring that even the busiest of us can enjoy a taste of Mediterranean life without spending hours in the kitchen.

This chapter is designed not just to instruct but to inspire you to embrace the joy of simple cooking. As we explore these various recipes, remember that each dish is more than just food; it's a story of the Mediterranean lifestyle a celebration of health, simplicity, and community. Let these dishes bring a touch of Mediterranean magic into your kitchen, proving once again that sometimes, less truly is more.

4.1 5-INGREDIENT SOUP RECIPES

CREAMY TOMATO BASIL SOUP

PREPARATION TIME: 10 min

COOKING TIME: 20 min

MODE OF COOKING: Simmering

SERVINGS: 4

INGREDIENTS:

- 2 cups canned crushed tomatoes
- 1 cup vegetable broth
- 1/2 cup heavy cream
- 2 Tbsp olive oil
- Fresh basil leaves, chopped

DIRECTIONS:

1. Heat olive oil in a large pot over medium heat.
2. Add the crushed tomatoes and vegetable broth, stirring to combine.
3. Bring to a simmer and cook for 15 minutes.
4. Stir in the heavy cream and cook for an additional 5 minutes.
5. Remove from heat and stir in chopped basil leaves before serving.

TIPS:

- Serve with crusty bread for a hearty meal.
- Garnish with additional basil leaves for extra flavor.

N.V.: Calories: 180, Fat: 14g, Carbs: 11g, Protein: 3g, Sugar: 7g, Sodium: 450mg, Potassium: 400mg, Cholesterol: 35mg

GREEK LEMON CHICKEN SOUP

PREPARATION TIME: 10 min

COOKING TIME: 20 min

MODE OF COOKING: Simmering

SERVINGS: 4

INGREDIENTS:

- 1 lb. chicken breast, diced
- 4 cups chicken broth
- 1/2 cup orzo pasta
- 1 lemon, juiced
- Fresh dill, chopped

DIRECTIONS:

1. In a large pot, bring the chicken broth to a boil.
2. Add diced chicken and orzo pasta, reducing heat to a simmer.
3. Cook for 15 minutes, until the chicken is cooked through and the pasta is tender.
4. Stir in lemon juice and chopped dill.

5. Simmer for an additional 5 minutes before serving.

TIPS:

- Serve with a side salad for a complete meal.
- Add lemon zest for an extra burst of flavor.

N.V.: Calories: 210, Fat: 3g, Carbs: 22g, Protein: 22g, Sugar: 1g, Sodium: 650mg, Potassium: 300mg, Cholesterol: 50mg

HEARTY LENTIL SOUP

PREPARATION TIME: 10 min

COOKING TIME: 30 min

MODE OF COOKING: Simmering

SERVINGS: 4

INGREDIENTS:

- 1 cup dried lentils
- 4 cups vegetable broth
- 1 cup diced tomatoes
- 1 onion, chopped
- 2 Tbsp olive oil

DIRECTIONS:

1. Heat olive oil in a large pot over medium heat.
2. Add chopped onion and cook until translucent, about 5 minutes.
3. Stir in lentils, diced tomatoes, and vegetable broth.
4. Bring to a boil, then reduce heat and simmer for 25 minutes, until lentils are tender.
5. Season with salt and pepper to taste before serving.

TIPS:

- Serve with a dollop of Greek yogurt for added creaminess.
- Add chopped spinach for extra nutrients.

N.V.: Calories: 250, Fat: 7g, Carbs: 38g, Protein: 14g, Sugar: 6g, Sodium: 500mg, Potassium: 650mg, Cholesterol: 0mg

SIMPLE CHICKPEA SOUP

PREPARATION TIME: 10 min

COOKING TIME: 20 min

MODE OF COOKING: Simmering

SERVINGS: 4

INGREDIENTS:

- 2 cups cooked chickpeas
- 4 cups vegetable broth
- 1 onion, chopped
- 2 Tbsp olive oil
- Fresh parsley, chopped

DIRECTIONS:

1. Heat olive oil in a large pot over medium heat.
2. Add chopped onion and cook until translucent, about 5 minutes.
3. Add chickpeas and vegetable broth, bringing to a boil.
4. Reduce heat and simmer for 15 minutes.
5. Blend half the soup for a creamier texture, then mix back in.
6. Garnish with chopped parsley before serving.

TIPS:

- Serve with a squeeze of lemon juice for a refreshing twist.
- Add a pinch of cumin for extra warmth.

N.V.: Calories: 220, Fat: 7g, Carbs: 32g, Protein: 8g, Sugar: 4g, Sodium: 500mg, Potassium: 400mg, Cholesterol: 0mg

ZUCCHINI AND MINT SOUP

PREPARATION TIME: 10 min

COOKING TIME: 20 min

MODE OF COOKING: Simmering

SERVINGS: 4

INGREDIENTS:

- 4 zucchinis, chopped
- 4 cups vegetable broth
- 1 onion, chopped
- 2 Tbsp olive oil
- Fresh mint leaves, chopped

DIRECTIONS:

1. Heat olive oil in a large pot over medium heat.
2. Add chopped onion and cook until translucent, about 5 minutes.
3. Add chopped zucchinis and vegetable broth, bringing to a boil.
4. Reduce heat and simmer for 15 minutes until zucchinis are tender.
5. Blend the soup until smooth.
6. Stir in chopped mint leaves before serving.

TIPS:

- Serve with a dollop of Greek yogurt for added creaminess.
- Garnish with extra mint leaves for a fresh finish.

N.V.: Calories: 150, Fat: 7g, Carbs: 20g, Protein: 3g, Sugar: 7g, Sodium: 450mg, Potassium: 550mg, Cholesterol: 0mg

ROASTED RED PEPPER SOUP

PREPARATION TIME: 10 min

COOKING TIME: 30 min

MODE OF COOKING: Simmering

SERVINGS: 4

INGREDIENTS:

- 4 roasted red peppers, chopped
- 4 cups vegetable broth
- 1 onion, chopped
- 2 Tbsp olive oil
- Fresh basil leaves, chopped

DIRECTIONS:

1. Heat olive oil in a large pot over medium heat.
2. Add chopped onion and cook until translucent, about 5 minutes.
3. Add chopped roasted red peppers and vegetable broth, bringing to a boil.
4. Reduce heat and simmer for 20 minutes.
5. Blend the soup until smooth.
6. Stir in chopped basil leaves before serving.

TIPS:

- Serve with a sprinkle of feta cheese for added flavor.
- Add a pinch of smoked paprika for a deeper taste.

N.V.: Calories: 160, Fat: 7g, Carbs: 22g, Protein: 2g, Sugar: 10g, Sodium: 500mg, Potassium: 500mg, Cholesterol: 0mg

TUSCAN WHITE BEAN SOUP

PREPARATION TIME: 10 min

COOKING TIME: 25 min

MODE OF COOKING: Simmering

SERVINGS: 4

INGREDIENTS:

- 2 cups cooked cannellini beans
- 4 cups vegetable broth
- 1 onion, chopped
- 2 cloves garlic, minced
- 2 Tbsp olive oil

DIRECTIONS:

1. Heat olive oil in a large pot over medium heat.
2. Add chopped onion and minced garlic, cooking until softened, about 5 minutes.
3. Add cannellini beans and vegetable broth, bringing to a boil.
4. Reduce heat and simmer for 20 minutes.
5. Blend half the soup for a creamy texture, then mix back in.

TIPS:

- Serve with a drizzle of olive oil and a sprinkle of fresh herbs.
- Add a squeeze of lemon juice for brightness.

N.V.: Calories: 220, Fat: 7g, Carbs: 30g, Protein: 8g, Sugar: 2g, Sodium: 450mg, Potassium: 600mg, Cholesterol: 0mg

MEDITERRANEAN FISH SOUP

PREPARATION TIME: 10 min

COOKING TIME: 20 min

MODE OF COOKING: Simmering

SERVINGS: 4

INGREDIENTS:

- 1 lb. white fish fillets, cut into chunks
- 4 cups fish broth
- 1 cup diced tomatoes
- 1 onion, chopped
- 2 Tbsp olive oil

DIRECTIONS:

1. Heat olive oil in a large pot over medium heat.
2. Add chopped onion and cook until softened, about 5 minutes.
3. Add diced tomatoes and fish broth, bringing to a boil.
4. Reduce heat and simmer for 10 minutes.
5. Add fish chunks and cook until fish is opaque, about 5 minutes.

TIPS:

- Serve with crusty bread to soak up the broth.
- Add fresh herbs like parsley for garnish.

N.V.: Calories: 200, Fat: 7g, Carbs: 8g, Protein: 25g, Sugar: 4g, Sodium: 600mg, Potassium: 800mg, Cholesterol: 60mg

CARROT AND GINGER SOUP

PREPARATION TIME: 10 min

COOKING TIME: 20 min

MODE OF COOKING: Simmering

SERVINGS: 4

INGREDIENTS:

- 4 large carrots, chopped
- 4 cups vegetable broth
- 1 onion, chopped
- 2 Tbsp olive oil
- 1 Tbsp grated fresh ginger

DIRECTIONS:

1. Heat olive oil in a large pot over medium heat.
2. Add chopped onion and cook until softened, about 5 minutes.
3. Add chopped carrots, grated ginger, and vegetable broth, bringing to a boil.
4. Reduce heat and simmer for 20 minutes, until carrots are tender.
5. Blend the soup until smooth.

TIPS:

- Serve with a dollop of Greek yogurt for creaminess.
- Garnish with fresh herbs like cilantro.

N.V.: Calories: 160, Fat: 7g, Carbs: 22g, Protein: 2g, Sugar: 10g, Sodium: 450mg, Potassium: 600mg, Cholesterol: 0mg

SPINACH AND POTATO SOUP

PREPARATION TIME: 10 min

COOKING TIME: 20 min

MODE OF COOKING: Simmering

SERVINGS: 4

INGREDIENTS:

- 4 cups spinach leaves
- 2 large potatoes, peeled and chopped
- 4 cups vegetable broth
- 1 onion, chopped
- 2 Tbsp olive oil

DIRECTIONS:

1. Heat olive oil in a large pot over medium heat.
2. Add chopped onion and cook until softened, about 5 minutes.
3. Add chopped potatoes and vegetable broth, bringing to a boil.
4. Reduce heat and simmer for 15 minutes, until potatoes are tender.
5. Add spinach leaves and cook for an additional 5 minutes.
6. Blend the soup until smooth.

TIPS:

- Serve with a sprinkle of nutmeg for added flavor.
- Garnish with a swirl of cream.

N.V.: Calories: 180, Fat: 7g, Carbs: 28g, Protein: 4g, Sugar: 4g, Sodium: 450mg, Potassium: 900mg, Cholesterol: 0mg

MEDITERRANEAN LENTIL AND SPINACH SOUP

PREPARATION TIME: 10 min

COOKING TIME: 30 min

MODE OF COOKING: Simmering

SERVINGS: 4

INGREDIENTS:

- 1 cup lentils
- 4 cups vegetable broth
- 2 cups fresh spinach
- 1 onion, chopped
- 2 Tbsp olive oil

DIRECTIONS:

1. Heat olive oil in a large pot over medium heat.
2. Add chopped onion and cook until softened, about 5 minutes.
3. Add lentils and vegetable broth, bringing to a boil.
4. Reduce heat and simmer for 25 minutes, until lentils are tender.
5. Add fresh spinach and cook for an additional 5 minutes.

TIPS:

- Serve with a drizzle of balsamic vinegar.
- Add a sprinkle of feta cheese for extra flavor.

N.V.: Calories: 210, Fat: 7g, Carbs: 30g, Protein: 9g, Sugar: 4g, Sodium: 450mg, Potassium: 800mg, Cholesterol: 0mg

RED LENTIL AND TOMATO SOUP

PREPARATION TIME: 10 min

COOKING TIME: 25 min

MODE OF COOKING: Simmering

SERVINGS: 4

INGREDIENTS:

- 1 cup red lentils
- 4 cups vegetable broth
- 1 cup diced tomatoes
- 1 onion, chopped
- 2 Tbsp olive oil

DIRECTIONS:

1. Heat olive oil in a large pot over medium heat.
2. Add chopped onion and cook until softened, about 5 minutes.
3. Add red lentils, diced tomatoes, and vegetable broth, bringing to a boil.
4. Reduce heat and simmer for 20 minutes, until lentils are tender.
5. Blend the soup for a smoother texture if desired.

TIPS:

- Serve with a sprinkle of fresh parsley.
- Add a squeeze of lemon juice for brightness.

N.V.: Calories: 230, Fat: 7g, Carbs: 32g, Protein: 12g, Sugar: 6g, Sodium: 450mg, Potassium: 700mg, Cholesterol: 0mg

GREEK SALAD

PREPARATION TIME: 10 min

COOKING TIME: 0 min

MODE OF COOKING: No-cook

SERVINGS: 4

INGREDIENTS:

- 2 cups cherry tomatoes, halved
- 1 cucumber, sliced
- 1/2 red onion, thinly sliced
- 1/2 cup kalamata olives
- 1/2 cup feta cheese, crumbled

DIRECTIONS:

1. In a large bowl, combine cherry tomatoes, cucumber, red onion, and kalamata olives.
2. Toss gently to mix.
3. Sprinkle feta cheese on top.
4. Serve immediately or chill for 30 minutes to let flavors meld.

TIPS:

- Drizzle with a bit of olive oil and a squeeze of lemon for extra flavor.
- Add fresh herbs like oregano or parsley for a fragrant touch.

N.V.: Calories: 120, Fat: 9g, Carbs: 8g, Protein: 3g, Sugar: 4g, Sodium: 350mg, Potassium: 350mg, Cholesterol: 15mg

CAPRESE SALAD

PREPARATION TIME: 10 min

COOKING TIME: 0 min

MODE OF COOKING: No-cook

SERVINGS: 4

INGREDIENTS:

- 3 large tomatoes, sliced
- 1 cup fresh mozzarella, sliced
- Fresh basil leaves
- 2 Tbsp olive oil
- 1 Tbsp balsamic glaze

DIRECTIONS:

1. Arrange tomato slices and mozzarella slices alternately on a serving platter.
2. Tuck fresh basil leaves between the tomato and mozzarella slices.
3. Drizzle with olive oil and balsamic glaze.
4. Serve immediately.

TIPS:

- Use heirloom tomatoes for a burst of color and flavor.
- Add a sprinkle of sea salt and cracked black pepper for seasoning.

N.V.: Calories: 200, Fat: 15g, Carbs: 8g, Protein: 10g, Sugar: 4g, Sodium: 200mg, Potassium: 400mg, Cholesterol: 25mg

MEDITERRANEAN QUINOA SALAD

PREPARATION TIME: 10 min

COOKING TIME: 15 min

MODE OF COOKING: Boiling

SERVINGS: 4

INGREDIENTS:

- 1 cup quinoa
- 2 cups water
- 1/2 cup cherry tomatoes, halved
- 1/4 cup kalamata olives, sliced
- 1/4 cup feta cheese, crumbled

DIRECTIONS:

1. Rinse quinoa under cold water.
2. In a medium saucepan, combine quinoa and water, and bring to a boil.
3. Reduce heat, cover, and simmer for 15 minutes, until quinoa is tender and water is absorbed.
4. Let quinoa cool slightly.
5. In a large bowl, combine quinoa, cherry tomatoes, kalamata olives, and feta cheese.
6. Toss gently to mix.

TIPS:

- Add a drizzle of lemon juice and olive oil for extra flavor.
- Chill the salad for 30 minutes before serving for a refreshing taste.

N.V.: Calories: 180, Fat: 8g, Carbs: 22g, Protein: 6g, Sugar: 2g, Sodium: 250mg, Potassium: 300mg, Cholesterol: 15mg

CUCUMBER AND MINT SALAD

PREPARATION TIME: 10 min

COOKING TIME: 0 min

MODE OF COOKING: No-cook

SERVINGS: 4

INGREDIENTS:

- 2 large cucumbers, thinly sliced
- 1/2 red onion, thinly sliced
- 1/4 cup fresh mint leaves, chopped
- 2 Tbsp olive oil
- 1 Tbsp lemon juice

DIRECTIONS:

1. In a large bowl, combine cucumbers, red onion, and fresh mint.
2. Drizzle with olive oil and lemon juice.
3. Toss gently to mix.
4. Serve immediately.

TIPS:

- Add a sprinkle of salt and pepper for seasoning.
- Chill the salad for 15 minutes before serving for a refreshing taste.

N.V.: Calories: 80, Fat: 7g, Carbs: 5g, Protein: 1g, Sugar: 2g, Sodium: 10mg, Potassium: 200mg, Cholesterol: 0mg

ARUGULA AND PARMESAN SALAD

PREPARATION TIME: 5 min

COOKING TIME: 0 min

MODE OF COOKING: No-cook

SERVINGS: 4

INGREDIENTS:

- 4 cups fresh arugula
- 1/4 cup shaved Parmesan cheese
- 2 Tbsp olive oil
- 1 Tbsp lemon juice
- Salt and pepper to taste

DIRECTIONS:

1. In a large bowl, combine arugula and shaved Parmesan cheese.
2. Drizzle with olive oil and lemon juice.
3. Season with salt and pepper.
4. Toss gently to mix.
5. Serve immediately.

TIPS:

- Add toasted pine nuts for extra crunch.
- Use a vegetable peeler to shave Parmesan cheese for perfect slices.

N.V.: Calories: 100, Fat: 9g, Carbs: 2g, Protein: 3g, Sugar: 0g, Sodium: 150mg, Potassium: 150mg, Cholesterol: 5mg

MEDITERRANEAN CHICKPEA SALAD

PREPARATION TIME: 10 min

COOKING TIME: 0 min

MODE OF COOKING: No-cook

SERVINGS: 4

INGREDIENTS:

- 1 can chickpeas, drained and rinsed
- 1/2 cup cherry tomatoes, halved
- 1/4 cup kalamata olives, sliced
- 1/4 cup feta cheese, crumbled
- 2 Tbsp olive oil

DIRECTIONS:

1. In a large bowl, combine chickpeas, cherry tomatoes, kalamata olives, and feta cheese.
2. Drizzle with olive oil.
3. Toss gently to mix.
4. Serve immediately or chill for 30 minutes to let flavors meld.

TIPS:

- Add a squeeze of lemon juice for extra freshness.
- Serve with whole grain pita for a complete meal.

N.V.: Calories: 200, Fat: 10g, Carbs: 22g, Protein: 6g, Sugar: 2g, Sodium: 300mg, Potassium: 300mg, Cholesterol: 15mg

WATERMELON AND FETA SALAD

PREPARATION TIME: 10 min

COOKING TIME: 0 min

MODE OF COOKING: No-cook

SERVINGS: 4

INGREDIENTS:

- 4 cups watermelon, cubed
- 1/2 cup feta cheese, crumbled
- 1/4 cup fresh mint leaves, chopped
- 2 Tbsp olive oil
- 1 Tbsp balsamic vinegar

DIRECTIONS:

1. In a large bowl, combine watermelon cubes and crumbled feta cheese.
2. Add chopped mint leaves.
3. Drizzle with olive oil and balsamic vinegar.
4. Toss gently to combine and serve immediately.

TIPS:

- Serve chilled for a refreshing summer treat.
- Garnish with additional mint leaves for extra flavor.

N.V.: Calories: 150, Fat: 10g, Carbs: 12g, Protein: 3g, Sugar: 10g, Sodium: 150mg, Potassium: 300mg, Cholesterol: 10mg

ROASTED BEET AND ORANGE SALAD

PREPARATION TIME: 10 min

COOKING TIME: 0 min

MODE OF COOKING: No-cook

SERVINGS: 4

INGREDIENTS:

- 4 roasted beets, sliced
- 2 oranges, segmented
- 1/4 cup goat cheese, crumbled
- 2 Tbsp olive oil
- Fresh arugula leaves

DIRECTIONS:

1. Arrange sliced roasted beets and orange segments on a platter.
2. Sprinkle with crumbled goat cheese.
3. Drizzle with olive oil.
4. Garnish with fresh arugula leaves and serve immediately.

TIPS:

- Roast the beets ahead of time to save preparation time.
- Add a sprinkle of salt and pepper for seasoning.

N.V.: Calories: 170, Fat: 10g, Carbs: 18g, Protein: 4g, Sugar: 12g, Sodium: 150mg, Potassium: 400mg, Cholesterol: 5mg

PANZANELLA SALAD

PREPARATION TIME: 10 min

COOKING TIME: 0 min

MODE OF COOKING: No-cook

SERVINGS: 4

INGREDIENTS:

- 2 cups cherry tomatoes, halved
- 1 cucumber, sliced
- 1/2 red onion, thinly sliced
- 2 cups stale bread cubes
- 1/4 cup basil leaves, chopped

DIRECTIONS:

1. In a large bowl, combine cherry tomatoes, cucumber, red onion, and bread cubes.
2. Add chopped basil leaves.
3. Toss gently to mix.
4. Let sit for 10 minutes to allow the bread to soak up the juices before serving.

TIPS:

- Use a mix of colorful tomatoes for a vibrant salad.
- Drizzle with olive oil and vinegar for extra flavor.

N.V.: Calories: 200, Fat: 5g, Carbs: 32g, Protein: 6g, Sugar: 8g, Sodium: 300mg, Potassium: 400mg, Cholesterol: 0mg

AVOCADO AND TOMATO SALAD

PREPARATION TIME: 10 min

COOKING TIME: 0 min

MODE OF COOKING: No-cook

SERVINGS: 4

INGREDIENTS:

- 2 avocados, diced
- 2 cups cherry tomatoes, halved
- 1/4 cup red onion, finely chopped
- 2 Tbsp lime juice
- Fresh cilantro leaves, chopped

DIRECTIONS:

1. In a large bowl, combine diced avocados, cherry tomatoes, and chopped red onion.
2. Drizzle with lime juice.
3. Add chopped cilantro leaves.
4. Toss gently to combine and serve immediately.

TIPS:

- Serve with tortilla chips for a fun appetizer.
- Add a pinch of salt and pepper for seasoning.

N.V.: Calories: 180, Fat: 15g, Carbs: 12g, Protein: 2g, Sugar: 4g, Sodium: 10mg, Potassium: 500mg, Cholesterol: 0mg

MEDITERRANEAN FARRO SALAD

PREPARATION TIME: 10 min

COOKING TIME: 20 min

MODE OF COOKING: Boiling

SERVINGS: 4

INGREDIENTS:

- 1 cup farro
- 2 cups vegetable broth
- 1/2 cup cherry tomatoes, halved
- 1/4 cup kalamata olives, sliced
- 2 Tbsp olive oil

DIRECTIONS:

1. In a medium saucepan, combine farro and vegetable broth, and bring to a boil.
2. Reduce heat, cover, and simmer for 20 minutes, until farro is tender.
3. Let farro cool slightly.
4. In a large bowl, combine cooked farro, cherry tomatoes, kalamata olives, and olive oil.
5. Toss gently to mix and serve.

TIPS:

- Add a squeeze of lemon juice for extra brightness.
- Serve chilled or at room temperature.

N.V.: Calories: 200, Fat: 8g, Carbs: 28g, Protein: 5g, Sugar: 2g, Sodium: 200mg, Potassium: 300mg, Cholesterol: 0mg

SPINACH AND STRAWBERRY SALAD

PREPARATION TIME: 10 min

COOKING TIME: 0 min

MODE OF COOKING: No-cook

SERVINGS: 4

INGREDIENTS:

- 4 cups baby spinach
- 1 cup strawberries, sliced
- 1/4 cup goat cheese, crumbled
- 2 Tbsp balsamic vinegar
- 2 Tbsp olive oil

DIRECTIONS:

1. In a large bowl, combine baby spinach and sliced strawberries.
2. Sprinkle with crumbled goat cheese.
3. Drizzle with balsamic vinegar and olive oil.
4. Toss gently to mix and serve immediately.

TIPS:

- Add toasted nuts for extra crunch.
- Use a balsamic reduction for a sweeter dressing.

N.V.: Calories: 160, Fat: 12g, Carbs: 12g, Protein: 4g, Sugar: 8g, Sodium: 150mg, Potassium: 300mg, Cholesterol: 5mg

Imagine stepping into a vibrant Mediterranean market: stalls brimming with colorful, fresh vegetables under the warm, inviting sun. Each turn unveils ingredients that are not only a feast for the eyes but also promise a bounty of health benefits. This is the spirit that Chapter 6: Veggie Dishes seeks to capture and bring to your kitchen.

Vegetables are the unsung heroes of the Mediterranean diet, providing a tapestry of flavors and textures that make every meal both nutritious and enticing. With only five ingredients, each recipe in this chapter is designed to celebrate the natural goodness of vegetables, transformed into dishes that will appeal to everyone at your table, from the youngest to the oldest.

In Mediterranean cultures, preparing and sharing meals is as much about nourishment as it is about connection. The recipes you'll find here are steeped in this tradition, offering simple yet innovative ways to turn everyday vegetables into culinary masterpieces. Picture yourself creating a crisp, refreshing salad with ripe tomatoes and crunchy cucumbers, brought to life with a drizzle of olive oil and a sprinkle of sea salt minimal ingredients for maximum pleasure.

Beyond the simplicity, these veggie dishes are adaptable. I understand that sourcing specific ingredients can sometimes be a challenge, so I've included tips for substitutions that maintain the integrity and flavor of each dish. Whether it's swapping spinach for kale or using a different herb blend, these modifications ensure that you can enjoy Mediterranean veggie dishes regardless of where you live or what's in your pantry.

Moreover, embracing vegetables in your diet is a step toward sustained health and vitality, echoing the longevity of Mediterranean populations. This chapter is not just about recipes; it's about transforming your approach to cooking and eating. It encourages you to slow down, savor each bite, and appreciate the natural richness of the Earth's bounty.

Let these recipes be your guide to a healthier, happier way of eating, one delicious vegetable dish at a time.

ROASTED EGGPLANT WITH TAHINI SAUCE

PREPARATION TIME: 10 min

COOKING TIME: 25 min

MODE OF COOKING: Roasting

SERVINGS: 4

INGREDIENTS:

- 2 large eggplants, sliced
- 2 Tbsp olive oil
- 1/4 cup tahini
- Juice of 1 lemon
- Fresh parsley, chopped

DIRECTIONS:

1. Preheat oven to 400°F (200°C).
2. Arrange eggplant slices on a baking sheet and brush with olive oil.
3. Roast for 25 minutes, until golden and tender.
4. In a small bowl, mix tahini and lemon juice until smooth.
5. Drizzle tahini sauce over roasted eggplant and sprinkle with fresh parsley before serving.

TIPS:

- Serve as a side dish or over a bed of quinoa for a complete meal.
- Add a pinch of smoked paprika to the tahini sauce for extra flavor.

N.V.: Calories: 180, Fat: 12g, Carbs: 15g, Protein: 3g, Sugar: 3g, Sodium: 20mg, Potassium: 400mg, Cholesterol: 0mg

STUFFED BELL PEPPERS

PREPARATION TIME: 15 min

COOKING TIME: 30 min

MODE OF COOKING: Baking

SERVINGS: 4

INGREDIENTS:

- 4 bell peppers, halved and seeded
- 1 cup cooked quinoa
- 1/2 cup feta cheese, crumbled
- 1 cup cherry tomatoes, halved
- 2 Tbsp olive oil

DIRECTIONS:

1. Preheat oven to 375°F (190°C).
2. In a bowl, combine cooked quinoa, feta cheese, and cherry tomatoes.
3. Stuff each bell pepper half with the quinoa mixture.
4. Arrange stuffed peppers on a baking sheet, drizzle with olive oil, and bake for 30 minutes.
5. Serve warm.

TIPS:

- Use a mix of colored bell peppers for a vibrant presentation.
- Add chopped fresh herbs like basil or parsley for extra freshness.

N.V.: Calories: 210, Fat: 10g, Carbs: 25g, Protein: 6g, Sugar: 5g, Sodium: 220mg, Potassium: 500mg, Cholesterol: 15mg

SPINACH AND CHICKPEA STEW

PREPARATION TIME: 10 min

COOKING TIME: 20 min

MODE OF COOKING: Simmering

SERVINGS: 4

INGREDIENTS:

- 1 can chickpeas, drained and rinsed
- 4 cups fresh spinach
- 1 onion, chopped
- 2 cloves garlic, minced
- 2 Tbsp olive oil

DIRECTIONS:

1. Heat olive oil in a large pot over medium heat.
2. Add chopped onion and minced garlic, and sauté until softened, about 5 minutes.
3. Add chickpeas and cook for another 5 minutes.
4. Add fresh spinach and cook until wilted, about 5 minutes.
5. Season with salt and pepper to taste and serve.

TIPS:

- Serve over rice or couscous for a heartier meal.
- Add a squeeze of lemon juice for extra brightness.

N.V.: Calories: 150, Fat: 7g, Carbs: 16g, Protein: 5g, Sugar: 2g, Sodium: 240mg, Potassium: 400mg, Cholesterol: 0mg

MEDITERRANEAN CAULIFLOWER RICE

PREPARATION TIME: 10 min

COOKING TIME: 10 min

MODE OF COOKING: Sautéing

SERVINGS: 4

INGREDIENTS:

- 1 head cauliflower, grated
- 1/4 cup sun-dried tomatoes, chopped
- 2 cloves garlic, minced
- 2 Tbsp olive oil
- Fresh basil leaves, chopped

DIRECTIONS:

1. Heat olive oil in a large skillet over medium heat.
2. Add minced garlic and cook until fragrant, about 1 minute.
3. Add grated cauliflower and cook for 5 minutes, stirring occasionally.
4. Stir in chopped sun-dried tomatoes and cook for another 2 minutes.
5. Garnish with fresh basil leaves and serve.

TIPS:

- Use frozen riced cauliflower for a quicker prep time.
- Add a sprinkle of Parmesan cheese for extra flavor.

N.V.: Calories: 100, Fat: 7g, Carbs: 7g, Protein: 2g, Sugar: 3g, Sodium: 150mg, Potassium: 300mg, Cholesterol: 0mg

ROASTED ZUCCHINI WITH PARMESAN

PREPARATION TIME: 5 min

COOKING TIME: 20 min

MODE OF COOKING: Roasting

SERVINGS: 4

INGREDIENTS:

- 4 zucchinis, sliced
- 2 Tbsp olive oil
- 1/4 cup grated Parmesan cheese
- 1 tsp dried oregano
- Salt and pepper to taste

DIRECTIONS:

1. Preheat oven to 400°F (200°C).
2. Arrange zucchini slices on a baking sheet and drizzle with olive oil.
3. Sprinkle with grated Parmesan cheese, dried oregano, salt, and pepper.
4. Roast for 20 minutes, until golden and tender.
5. Serve warm.

TIPS:

- Add a squeeze of lemon juice before serving for extra brightness.
- Garnish with fresh parsley for a pop of color.

N.V.: Calories: 130, Fat: 9g, Carbs: 8g, Protein: 4g, Sugar: 4g, Sodium: 150mg, Potassium: 450mg, Cholesterol: 5mg

BAKED FETA WITH CHERRY TOMATOES

PREPARATION TIME: 5 min

COOKING TIME: 25 min

MODE OF COOKING: Baking

SERVINGS: 4

INGREDIENTS:

- 1 block of feta cheese
- 2 cups cherry tomatoes
- 2 Tbsp olive oil
- 2 cloves garlic, sliced
- Fresh thyme leaves

DIRECTIONS:

1. Preheat oven to 375°F (190°C).
2. Place the block of feta in the center of a baking dish.
3. Surround the feta with cherry tomatoes and garlic slices.
4. Drizzle everything with olive oil and sprinkle with fresh thyme leaves.
5. Bake for 25 minutes, until the feta is soft and the tomatoes are blistered.
6. Serve warm with crusty bread.

TIPS:

- Use a mix of cherry tomatoes for a colorful presentation.
- Add a drizzle of honey over the feta before baking for a touch of sweetness.

N.V.: Calories: 200, Fat: 16g, Carbs: 6g, Protein: 7g, Sugar: 4g, Sodium: 450mg, Potassium: 200mg, Cholesterol: 25mg

GRILLED ASPARAGUS WITH LEMON

PREPARATION TIME: 5 min

COOKING TIME: 10 min

MODE OF COOKING: Grilling

SERVINGS: 4

INGREDIENTS:

- 1 lb. asparagus, trimmed
- 2 Tbsp olive oil
- Juice of 1 lemon
- 2 cloves garlic, minced
- Salt and pepper to taste

DIRECTIONS:

1. Preheat grill to medium-high heat.
2. Toss asparagus with olive oil, minced garlic, salt, and pepper.
3. Grill asparagus for 5-7 minutes, turning occasionally, until tender and slightly charred.
4. Drizzle with lemon juice before serving.

TIPS:

- Serve with grilled fish or chicken for a complete meal.
- Add a sprinkle of Parmesan cheese for extra flavor.

N.V.: Calories: 60, Fat: 5g, Carbs: 4g, Protein: 2g, Sugar: 1g, Sodium: 150mg, Potassium: 230mg, Cholesterol: 0mg

GARLIC GREEN BEANS

PREPARATION TIME: 5 min

COOKING TIME: 10 min

MODE OF COOKING: Sautéing

SERVINGS: 4

INGREDIENTS:

- 1 lb. green beans, trimmed
- 2 Tbsp olive oil
- 3 cloves garlic, minced
- Juice of 1 lemon
- Salt and pepper to taste

DIRECTIONS:

1. Heat olive oil in a large skillet over medium heat.
2. Add minced garlic and cook until fragrant, about 1 minute.
3. Add green beans and sauté for 7-8 minutes, until tender-crisp.
4. Drizzle with lemon juice and season with salt and pepper before serving.

TIPS:

- Add red pepper flakes for a spicy kick.
- Top with toasted almonds for extra crunch.

N.V.: Calories: 80, Fat: 5g, Carbs: 8g, Protein: 2g, Sugar: 2g, Sodium: 200mg, Potassium: 250mg, Cholesterol: 0mg

BALSAMIC GLAZED CARROTS

PREPARATION TIME: 5 min

COOKING TIME: 20 min

MODE OF COOKING: Roasting

SERVINGS: 4

INGREDIENTS:

- 1 lb. carrots, peeled and sliced
- 2 Tbsp olive oil
- 2 Tbsp balsamic vinegar
- 1 Tbsp honey
- Salt and pepper to taste

DIRECTIONS:

1. Preheat oven to 400°F (200°C).
2. Toss carrots with olive oil, balsamic vinegar, honey, salt, and pepper.
3. Spread carrots on a baking sheet in a single layer.
4. Roast for 20 minutes, stirring halfway through, until tender and caramelized.

TIPS:

- Garnish with fresh thyme or parsley for added flavor.
- Use rainbow carrots for a colorful dish.

N.V.: Calories: 110, Fat: 5g, Carbs: 15g, Protein: 1g, Sugar: 10g, Sodium: 150mg, Potassium: 320mg, Cholesterol: 0mg

SAUTÉED MUSHROOMS WITH THYME

PREPARATION TIME: 5 min

COOKING TIME: 15 min

MODE OF COOKING: Sautéing

SERVINGS: 4

INGREDIENTS:

- 1 lb. mushrooms, sliced
- 2 Tbsp olive oil
- 2 cloves garlic, minced
- 1 Tbsp fresh thyme leaves
- Salt and pepper to taste

DIRECTIONS:

1. Heat olive oil in a large skillet over medium heat.
2. Add minced garlic and cook until fragrant, about 1 minute.
3. Add mushrooms and sauté for 10-12 minutes, until golden brown and tender.
4. Stir in fresh thyme leaves and season with salt and pepper before serving.

TIPS:

- Serve as a side dish or over toast for a simple meal.
- Add a splash of white wine for extra depth of flavor.

N.V.: Calories: 100, Fat: 7g, Carbs: 5g, Protein: 2g, Sugar: 1g, Sodium: 150mg, Potassium: 400mg, Cholesterol: 0mg

ROASTED BRUSSELS SPROUTS

PREPARATION TIME: 5 min

COOKING TIME: 20 min

MODE OF COOKING: Roasting

SERVINGS: 4

INGREDIENTS:

- 1 lb. Brussels sprouts, halved
- 2 Tbsp olive oil
- 1 Tbsp balsamic vinegar
- Salt and pepper to taste
- 1/4 cup Parmesan cheese, grated

DIRECTIONS:

1. Preheat oven to 400°F (200°C).
2. Toss Brussels sprouts with olive oil, balsamic vinegar, salt, and pepper.
3. Spread Brussels sprouts on a baking sheet in a single layer.
4. Roast for 20 minutes, until crispy and tender.
5. Sprinkle with grated Parmesan cheese before serving.

TIPS:

- Add a drizzle of honey for a sweet and savory flavor.
- Top with toasted nuts for added crunch.

N.V.: Calories: 120, Fat: 8g, Carbs: 10g, Protein: 4g, Sugar: 2g, Sodium: 200mg, Potassium: 400mg, Cholesterol: 5mg

MEDITERRANEAN STUFFED ZUCCHINI

PREPARATION TIME: 10 min

COOKING TIME: 25 min

MODE OF COOKING: Baking

SERVINGS: 4

INGREDIENTS:

- 4 zucchinis, halved and scooped
- 1 cup cherry tomatoes, diced
- 1/2 cup feta cheese, crumbled
- 2 cloves garlic, minced
- 2 Tbsp olive oil

DIRECTIONS:

1. Preheat oven to 375°F (190°C).
2. In a bowl, combine diced cherry tomatoes, crumbled feta cheese, minced garlic, and olive oil.
3. Fill zucchini halves with the tomato and feta mixture.
4. Place stuffed zucchinis on a baking sheet and bake for 25 minutes, until zucchini is tender.
5. Serve warm.

TIPS:

- Add fresh basil or oregano for extra flavor.
- Use a spoon to easily scoop out the zucchini flesh.

N.V.: Calories: 140, Fat: 10g, Carbs: 8g, Protein: 4g, Sugar: 4g, Sodium: 250mg, Potassium: 450mg, Cholesterol: 10mg

CHAPTER 5: SAUCES AND DIPS

Imagine standing in a bustling Mediterranean market, the air rich with the scents of ripe olives, fresh herbs, and citrus. They're not just mere ingredients; they're the soul of Mediterranean cuisine, often brought together in the simplest yet most transformative aspect of cooking: sauces and dips. In this chapter, we'll explore the art of using just five ingredients to craft flavorful accompaniments that can elevate a routine meal to a culinary adventure.

Sauces and dips in the Mediterranean diet do more than enhance flavor; they interweave history, culture, and nutrition in every spoonful. Each recipe in this section is a mini chronicle of Mediterranean life, where food is about sharing, health, and celebration. Whether it's a velvety yogurt tzatziki, a robust tomato salsa, or a vibrant basil pesto, the philosophy here is straightforward maximum flavor with minimal ingredients.

Consider, for instance, the classic Greek Tzatziki. With just yogurt, cucumber, garlic, olive oil, and dill, this dip doesn't just complement a dish; it transforms it, adding layers of refreshing, tangy, and creamy textures. Or take the Italian pesto, a blend of fresh basil, garlic, pine nuts, Parmesan, and olive oil simple ingredients that, when combined, pack a punch of lush, herbaceous vibrancy.

Creating these sauces and dips can be a delightful culinary exploration that doesn't burden your time nor your budget. They require minimal cooking, yet each one offers a healthful contribution to your dining table, aligning perfectly with your goals for better health and weight management. These recipes are crafted to help you navigate a hectic week, offering quick fixes that are both nourishing and delightful, proving that simplicity does not compromise taste or quality.

So, let's embark on this flavorful journey with our collection of saucy inspirations, where each recipe promises to deliver a taste of the Mediterranean, effortlessly brought into your kitchen and onto your plate. Here's to discovering that the essence of great flavor often lies in the humblest of pots.

5.1 5-INGREDIENT SAUCES AND DIPS

CLASSIC TZATZIKI SAUCE

PREPARATION TIME: 10 min

COOKING TIME: 0 min

MODE OF COOKING: No-cook

SERVINGS: 4

INGREDIENTS:

- 1 cup Greek yogurt
- 1 cucumber, grated and squeezed
- 2 cloves garlic, minced
- 1 Tbsp olive oil
- 1 Tbsp fresh dill, chopped

DIRECTIONS:

1. In a medium bowl, combine Greek yogurt, grated cucumber, minced garlic, olive oil, and fresh dill.
2. Mix well until all ingredients are thoroughly combined.
3. Serve immediately or refrigerate for an hour to let the flavors meld.

TIPS:

- Squeeze the grated cucumber well to remove excess moisture.
- Serve with pita bread or fresh vegetables.

N.V.: Calories: 80, Fat: 4g, Carbs: 5g, Protein: 5g, Sugar: 4g, Sodium: 50mg, Potassium: 150mg, Cholesterol: 5mg

SPICY HARISSA PASTE

PREPARATION TIME: 10 min

COOKING TIME: 5 min

MODE OF COOKING: Blending

SERVINGS: 4

INGREDIENTS:

- 2 roasted red peppers
- 2 cloves garlic
- 1 Tbsp olive oil
- 1 tsp ground cumin
- 1 tsp smoked paprika

DIRECTIONS:

1. In a food processor, combine roasted red peppers, garlic, olive oil, ground cumin, and smoked paprika.
2. Blend until smooth and well combined.
3. Adjust seasoning to taste and serve.

TIPS:

- Store in an airtight container in the fridge for up to a week.
- Use as a marinade for meats or a spread for sandwiches.

N.V.: Calories: 50, Fat: 4g, Carbs: 5g, Protein: 1g, Sugar: 3g, Sodium: 30mg, Potassium: 200mg, Cholesterol: 0mg

LEMON HERB VINAIGRETTE

PREPARATION TIME: 5 min

COOKING TIME: 0 min

MODE OF COOKING: No-cook

SERVINGS: 4

INGREDIENTS:

- 1/4 cup olive oil
- 2 Tbsp lemon juice
- 1 tsp Dijon mustard
- 1 clove garlic, minced
- 1 Tbsp fresh parsley, chopped

DIRECTIONS:

1. In a small bowl, whisk together olive oil, lemon juice, Dijon mustard, minced garlic, and fresh parsley.
2. Mix until well emulsified.
3. Serve immediately or refrigerate until ready to use.

TIPS:

- Shake well before each use if stored.
- Drizzle over salads or roasted vegetables.

N.V.: Calories: 120, Fat: 14g, Carbs: 1g, Protein: 0g, Sugar: 0g, Sodium: 40mg, Potassium: 10mg, Cholesterol: 0mg

ROASTED RED PEPPER HUMMUS

PREPARATION TIME: 10 min

COOKING TIME: 0 min

MODE OF COOKING: Blending

SERVINGS: 4

INGREDIENTS:

- 1 can chickpeas, drained and rinsed
- 1 roasted red pepper
- 2 Tbsp tahini
- 1 clove garlic, minced
- 2 Tbsp olive oil

DIRECTIONS:

1. In a food processor, combine chickpeas, roasted red pepper, tahini, minced garlic, and olive oil.
2. Blend until smooth and creamy.
3. Serve with pita bread or fresh vegetables.

TIPS:

- Adjust seasoning with salt and pepper to taste.
- Add a splash of lemon juice for extra brightness.

N.V.: Calories: 180, Fat: 10g, Carbs: 18g, Protein: 5g, Sugar: 1g, Sodium: 240mg, Potassium: 150mg, Cholesterol: 0mg

BASIL PESTO

PREPARATION TIME: 10 min

COOKING TIME: 0 min

MODE OF COOKING: Blending

SERVINGS: 4

INGREDIENTS:

- 2 cups fresh basil leaves
- 1/4 cup pine nuts
- 1/2 cup olive oil
- 1/4 cup Parmesan cheese, grated
- 2 cloves garlic

DIRECTIONS:

1. In a food processor, combine basil leaves, pine nuts, Parmesan cheese, and garlic.
2. Pulse until finely chopped.
3. With the processor running, slowly add olive oil until the mixture is smooth.
4. Serve immediately or store in the refrigerator.

TIPS:

- Use as a sauce for pasta or a spread for sandwiches.
- Add a squeeze of lemon juice for extra flavor.

N.V.: Calories: 200, Fat: 20g, Carbs: 3g, Protein: 3g, Sugar: 0g, Sodium: 150mg, Potassium: 100mg, Cholesterol: 5mg

OLIVE TAPENADE

PREPARATION TIME: 10 min

COOKING TIME: 0 min

MODE OF COOKING: Blending

SERVINGS: 4

INGREDIENTS:

- 1 cup kalamata olives, pitted
- 2 Tbsp capers
- 2 cloves garlic
- 2 Tbsp olive oil
- 1 Tbsp lemon juice

DIRECTIONS:

1. In a food processor, combine kalamata olives, capers, garlic, olive oil, and lemon juice.
2. Blend until the mixture is finely chopped but still has some texture.
3. Serve immediately with bread or crackers.

TIPS:

- Use as a spread for sandwiches or a topping for grilled meats.
- Store in an airtight container in the fridge for up to a week.

N.V.: Calories: 140, Fat: 14g, Carbs: 2g, Protein: 1g, Sugar: 0g, Sodium: 700mg, Potassium: 100mg, Cholesterol: 0mg

SUN-DRIED TOMATO PESTO

PREPARATION TIME: 10 min

COOKING TIME: 0 min

MODE OF COOKING: Blending

SERVINGS: 4

INGREDIENTS:

- 1 cup sun-dried tomatoes in oil, drained
- 1/4 cup Parmesan cheese, grated
- 1/4 cup pine nuts
- 2 cloves garlic
- 1/2 cup olive oil

DIRECTIONS:

1. In a food processor, combine sun-dried tomatoes, Parmesan cheese, pine nuts, and garlic.
2. Pulse until finely chopped.
3. With the processor running, slowly add olive oil until the mixture is smooth.
4. Serve immediately or store in the refrigerator.

TIPS:

- Use as a pasta sauce or spread on sandwiches.
- Add a splash of balsamic vinegar for extra flavor.

N.V.: Calories: 220, Fat: 20g, Carbs: 5g, Protein: 4g, Sugar: 2g, Sodium: 250mg, Potassium: 200mg, Cholesterol: 5mg

GARLIC AIOLI

PREPARATION TIME: 5 min

COOKING TIME: 0 min

MODE OF COOKING: No-cook

SERVINGS: 4

INGREDIENTS:

- 1/2 cup mayonnaise
- 2 cloves garlic, minced
- 1 Tbsp lemon juice
- 1 Tbsp olive oil
- Salt to taste

DIRECTIONS:

1. In a small bowl, combine mayonnaise, minced garlic, lemon juice, and olive oil.
2. Mix until well blended.
3. Season with salt to taste and serve.

TIPS:

- Serve as a dip for fries or vegetables.
- Use as a spread for sandwiches and burgers.

N.V.: Calories: 180, Fat: 20g, Carbs: 1g, Protein: 0g, Sugar: 0g, Sodium: 150mg, Potassium: 0mg, Cholesterol: 10mg

MINT YOGURT SAUCE

PREPARATION TIME: 5 min

COOKING TIME: 0 min

MODE OF COOKING: No-cook

SERVINGS: 4

INGREDIENTS:

- 1 cup Greek yogurt
- 1/4 cup fresh mint leaves, chopped
- 1 clove garlic, minced
- 1 Tbsp lemon juice
- Salt to taste

DIRECTIONS:

1. In a medium bowl, combine Greek yogurt, chopped mint leaves, minced garlic, and lemon juice.
2. Mix until well combined.
3. Season with salt to taste and serve.

TIPS:

- Serve with lamb or as a dip for vegetables.
- Add a pinch of cumin for extra flavor.

N.V.: Calories: 70, Fat: 2g, Carbs: 5g, Protein: 7g, Sugar: 4g, Sodium: 50mg, Potassium: 150mg, Cholesterol: 5mg

RED PEPPER COULIS

PREPARATION TIME: 10 min

COOKING TIME: 5 min

MODE OF COOKING: Blending

SERVINGS: 4

INGREDIENTS:

- 2 roasted red peppers
- 1 clove garlic
- 2 Tbsp olive oil
- 1 Tbsp balsamic vinegar
- Salt to taste

DIRECTIONS:

1. In a blender, combine roasted red peppers, garlic, olive oil, and balsamic vinegar.
2. Blend until smooth.
3. Season with salt to taste and serve.

TIPS:

- Serve as a sauce for grilled meats or fish.
- Use as a vibrant dip for vegetables.

N.V.: Calories: 80, Fat: 7g, Carbs: 5g, Protein: 1g, Sugar: 4g, Sodium: 50mg, Potassium: 150mg, Cholesterol: 0mg

TAHINI SAUCE

PREPARATION TIME: 5 min

COOKING TIME: 0 min

MODE OF COOKING: No-cook

SERVINGS: 4

INGREDIENTS:

- 1/2 cup tahini
- 1/4 cup water
- 1 Tbsp lemon juice
- 1 clove garlic, minced
- Salt to taste

DIRECTIONS:

1. In a small bowl, combine tahini, water, lemon juice, and minced garlic.
2. Mix until smooth and well combined.
3. Season with salt to taste and serve.

TIPS:

- Adjust the consistency by adding more water if needed.
- Use as a dressing for salads or a dip for vegetables.

N.V.: Calories: 120, Fat: 10g, Carbs: 5g, Protein: 3g, Sugar: 0g, Sodium: 40mg, Potassium: 100mg, Cholesterol: 0mg

SIMPLE TOMATO BRUSCHETTA

PREPARATION TIME: 10 min

COOKING TIME: 0 min

MODE OF COOKING: No-cook

SERVINGS: 4

INGREDIENTS:

- 4 ripe tomatoes, diced
- 2 cloves garlic, minced
- 1/4 cup fresh basil leaves, chopped
- 2 Tbsp olive oil
- Salt and pepper to taste

DIRECTIONS:

1. In a medium bowl, combine diced tomatoes, minced garlic, and chopped basil leaves.
2. Drizzle with olive oil and season with salt and pepper.
3. Toss gently to mix.
4. Serve immediately on toasted bread or crackers.

TIPS:

- Use a variety of heirloom tomatoes for extra flavor and color.
- Rub the toasted bread with a garlic clove before adding the tomato mixture for extra garlic flavor.

N.V.: Calories: 70, Fat: 5g, Carbs: 5g, Protein: 1g, Sugar: 3g, Sodium: 150mg, Potassium: 200mg, Cholesterol: 0mg

Imagine the fresh, brisk breeze of the Mediterranean caressing your face as you stroll through a bustling market by the sea. The stalls are vibrant with freshly caught fish, their silvery scales glistening under the warm sun, promising a bounty of flavors. This is the essence of Mediterranean seafood an integral part of a diet celebrated for its health benefits and delightful tastes. In this chapter, we journey through the simple yet exquisite world of seafood dishes that require no more than five key ingredients, embodying the true spirit of Mediterranean cooking.

Seafood is not only a staple in Mediterranean cuisine but also a source of high-quality protein and essential omega-3 fatty acids, known for improving heart health and enhancing brain function. Cooking with a limited number of components accentuates the natural flavors of the sea, transforming a humble meal into a gastronomic delight that nourishes both body and soul.

Here, we'll explore dishes that fuse tradition with modern simplicity, from a tender grilled octopus dressed in a fragrant olive oil and lemon dressing to succulent shrimp sizzled with garlic and a hint of chili. Each recipe is a love letter to the sea, designed to bring its freshness to your table, effortlessly.

The beauty of these recipes lies in their simplicity and versatility. Whether you're hosting a dinner party or looking for a quick midweek meal, the dishes we're about to discover are as easy to prepare as they are satisfying. You'll learn how to coax the richest flavors out of just a few ingredients embracing the very philosophy that makes the Mediterranean diet so beneficial and enduring.

Let's dive into the azure waters of Mediterranean cooking with enthusiasm and ease. Each page turned is a step closer to mastering the art of simple seafood cooking, ensuring you can enjoy a slice of Mediterranean life, no matter where you are in the world. Together, we'll make every meal a celebration of the sea's bountiful harvest.

6.1 5-INGREDIENT SEAFOOD RECIPES

GRILLED LEMON GARLIC SHRIMP

PREPARATION TIME: 10 min

COOKING TIME: 10 min

MODE OF COOKING: Grilling

SERVINGS: 4

INGREDIENTS:

- 1 lb. shrimp, peeled and deveined
- 2 Tbsp olive oil
- 3 cloves garlic, minced
- Juice of 1 lemon
- 1 Tbsp fresh parsley, chopped

DIRECTIONS:

1. In a bowl, combine olive oil, minced garlic, and lemon juice.
2. Add shrimp to the bowl and toss to coat.
3. Preheat grill to medium-high heat.
4. Thread shrimp onto skewers and grill for 3-4 minutes on each side, until pink and opaque.
5. Sprinkle with fresh parsley before serving.

TIPS:

- Serve with a side of grilled vegetables for a complete meal.
- Use wooden skewers soaked in water to prevent burning.

N.V.: Calories: 180, Fat: 9g, Carbs: 2g, Protein: 23g, Sugar: 0g, Sodium: 220mg, Potassium: 220mg, Cholesterol: 170mg

BAKED COD WITH TOMATOES AND OLIVES

PREPARATION TIME: 10 min

COOKING TIME: 20 min

MODE OF COOKING: Baking

SERVINGS: 4

INGREDIENTS:

- 4 cod fillets
- 2 cups cherry tomatoes, halved
- 1/2 cup kalamata olives, pitted and halved
- 2 Tbsp olive oil
- 1 tsp dried oregano

DIRECTIONS:

1. Preheat oven to 375°F (190°C).
2. Place cod fillets in a baking dish.
3. In a bowl, combine cherry tomatoes, kalamata olives, olive oil, and dried oregano.
4. Spoon the tomato mixture over the cod fillets.
5. Bake for 20 minutes, until the fish is flaky and cooked through.

TIPS:

- Serve with a side of rice or quinoa.
- Add a splash of white wine before baking for extra flavor.

N.V.: Calories: 220, Fat: 10g, Carbs: 6g, Protein: 28g, Sugar: 3g, Sodium: 350mg, Potassium: 600mg, Cholesterol: 70mg

PAN-SEARED SCALLOPS WITH BASIL PESTO

PREPARATION TIME: 10 min

COOKING TIME: 10 min

MODE OF COOKING: Searing

SERVINGS: 4

INGREDIENTS:

- 1 lb. sea scallops
- 2 Tbsp olive oil
- 1/2 cup basil pesto
- Juice of 1 lemon
- Salt and pepper to taste

DIRECTIONS:

1. Pat scallops dry and season with salt and pepper.
2. Heat olive oil in a large skillet over medium-high heat.
3. Add scallops and sear for 2-3 minutes on each side, until golden brown and cooked through.
4. Drizzle with lemon juice and serve with basil pesto on the side.

TIPS:

- Serve over a bed of arugula or mixed greens.
- Garnish with lemon zest for extra brightness.

N.V.: Calories: 250, Fat: 14g, Carbs: 4g, Protein: 24g, Sugar: 0g, Sodium: 400mg, Potassium: 450mg, Cholesterol: 50mg

MEDITERRANEAN TUNA SALAD

PREPARATION TIME: 10 min

COOKING TIME: 0 min

MODE OF COOKING: No-cook

SERVINGS: 4

INGREDIENTS:

- 2 cans tuna, drained
- 1/2 cup cherry tomatoes, halved
- 1/4 cup kalamata olives, sliced
- 2 Tbsp olive oil
- Juice of 1 lemon

DIRECTIONS:

1. In a large bowl, combine tuna, cherry tomatoes, and kalamata olives.
2. Drizzle with olive oil and lemon juice.
3. Toss gently to combine and serve.

TIPS:

- Serve with whole grain crackers or in lettuce wraps.
- Add fresh basil or parsley for extra flavor.

N.V.: Calories: 220, Fat: 12g, Carbs: 2g, Protein: 24g, Sugar: 0g, Sodium: 300mg, Potassium: 450mg, Cholesterol: 40mg

LEMON HERB GRILLED SALMON

PREPARATION TIME: 10 min

COOKING TIME: 15 min

MODE OF COOKING: Grilling

SERVINGS: 4

INGREDIENTS:

- 4 salmon fillets
- 2 Tbsp olive oil
- Juice of 1 lemon
- 2 cloves garlic, minced
- 1 Tbsp fresh dill, chopped

DIRECTIONS:

1. In a bowl, combine olive oil, lemon juice, minced garlic, and fresh dill.
2. Brush salmon fillets with the mixture.
3. Preheat grill to medium-high heat.
4. Grill salmon for 6-7 minutes on each side, until cooked through.
5. Serve immediately.

TIPS:

- Serve with a side of roasted vegetables or a salad.
- Garnish with lemon slices and additional dill.

N.V.: Calories: 300, Fat: 20g, Carbs: 2g, Protein: 25g, Sugar: 0g, Sodium: 90mg, Potassium: 700mg, Cholesterol: 70mg

GARLIC BUTTER SHRIMP

PREPARATION TIME: 10 min

COOKING TIME: 10 min

MODE OF COOKING: Sautéing

SERVINGS: 4

INGREDIENTS:

- 1 lb. shrimp, peeled and deveined
- 3 Tbsp butter
- 3 cloves garlic, minced
- Juice of 1 lemon
- Fresh parsley, chopped

DIRECTIONS:

1. Melt butter in a large skillet over medium heat.
2. Add minced garlic and sauté for 1 minute.
3. Add shrimp and cook for 3-4 minutes on each side, until pink and opaque.
4. Drizzle with lemon juice and sprinkle with fresh parsley before serving.

TIPS:

- Serve over pasta or rice for a complete meal.
- Add red pepper flakes for a spicy kick.

N.V.: Calories: 250, Fat: 15g, Carbs: 2g, Protein: 24g, Sugar: 0g, Sodium: 200mg, Potassium: 220mg, Cholesterol: 200mg

MEDITERRANEAN BAKED SHRIMP

PREPARATION TIME: 10 min

COOKING TIME: 15 min

MODE OF COOKING: Baking

SERVINGS: 4

INGREDIENTS:

- 1 lb. shrimp, peeled and deveined
- 1 cup cherry tomatoes, halved
- 1/2 cup kalamata olives, sliced
- 2 Tbsp olive oil
- 1 Tbsp fresh oregano, chopped

DIRECTIONS:

1. Preheat oven to 400°F (200°C).
2. In a baking dish, combine shrimp, cherry tomatoes, and kalamata olives.
3. Drizzle with olive oil and sprinkle with chopped oregano.
4. Bake for 15 minutes, until shrimp are pink and cooked through.
5. Serve immediately.

TIPS:

- Serve with crusty bread to soak up the juices.
- Garnish with fresh lemon wedges.

N.V.: Calories: 220, Fat: 10g, Carbs: 4g, Protein: 28g, Sugar: 2g, Sodium: 400mg, Potassium: 400mg, Cholesterol: 190mg

LEMON GARLIC GRILLED MACKEREL

PREPARATION TIME: 10 min

COOKING TIME: 15 min

MODE OF COOKING: Grilling

SERVINGS: 4

INGREDIENTS:

- 4 mackerel fillets
- 3 Tbsp olive oil
- 3 cloves garlic, minced
- Juice of 1 lemon
- Fresh parsley, chopped

DIRECTIONS:

1. In a bowl, combine olive oil, minced garlic, and lemon juice.
2. Brush mackerel fillets with the mixture.
3. Preheat grill to medium-high heat.
4. Grill mackerel for 6-7 minutes on each side, until cooked through.
5. Sprinkle with fresh parsley before serving.

TIPS:

- Serve with a side of steamed vegetables.
- Garnish with lemon wedges for extra flavor.

N.V.: Calories: 280, Fat: 18g, Carbs: 1g, Protein: 28g, Sugar: 0g, Sodium: 100mg, Potassium: 800mg, Cholesterol: 70mg

TOMATO BASIL SALMON

PREPARATION TIME: 10 min

COOKING TIME: 20 min

MODE OF COOKING: Baking

SERVINGS: 4

INGREDIENTS:

- 4 salmon fillets
- 2 cups cherry tomatoes, halved
- 2 Tbsp olive oil
- 2 cloves garlic, minced
- Fresh basil leaves, chopped

DIRECTIONS:

1. Preheat oven to 375°F (190°C).
2. Place salmon fillets in a baking dish.
3. In a bowl, combine cherry tomatoes, olive oil, and minced garlic.
4. Spoon the tomato mixture over the salmon fillets.
5. Bake for 20 minutes, until the salmon is cooked through.
6. Sprinkle with fresh basil leaves before serving.

TIPS:

- Serve with a side of quinoa or rice.
- Add a splash of balsamic vinegar for extra depth of flavor.

N.V.: Calories: 300, Fat: 20g, Carbs: 4g, Protein: 26g, Sugar: 2g, Sodium: 150mg, Potassium: 800mg, Cholesterol: 70mg

HERB-CRUSTED COD

PREPARATION TIME: 10 min

COOKING TIME: 15 min

MODE OF COOKING: Baking

SERVINGS: 4

INGREDIENTS:

- 4 cod fillets
- 1 cup breadcrumbs
- 2 Tbsp olive oil
- 2 cloves garlic, minced
- Fresh thyme leaves

DIRECTIONS:

1. Preheat oven to 400°F (200°C).
2. In a bowl, combine breadcrumbs, olive oil, minced garlic, and fresh thyme leaves.
3. Press the breadcrumb mixture onto the cod fillets.
4. Place the fillets on a baking sheet and bake for 15 minutes, until the fish is flaky and golden brown.
5. Serve immediately.

TIPS:

- Serve with a lemon wedge for added brightness.
- Pair with a side of roasted vegetables.

N.V.: Calories: 250, Fat: 12g, Carbs: 12g, Protein: 24g, Sugar: 1g, Sodium: 300mg, Potassium: 700mg, Cholesterol: 70mg

GRILLED SWORDFISH WITH ROSEMARY

PREPARATION TIME: 10 min

COOKING TIME: 15 min

MODE OF COOKING: Grilling

SERVINGS: 4

INGREDIENTS:

- 4 swordfish steaks
- 2 Tbsp olive oil
- Juice of 1 lemon
- 2 cloves garlic, minced
- 1 Tbsp fresh rosemary, chopped

DIRECTIONS:

1. In a bowl, combine olive oil, lemon juice, minced garlic, and chopped rosemary.
2. Brush swordfish steaks with the mixture.
3. Preheat grill to medium-high heat.
4. Grill swordfish for 6-7 minutes on each side, until cooked through.
5. Serve immediately.

TIPS:

- Serve with a fresh green salad.
- Garnish with additional rosemary sprigs.

N.V.: Calories: 320, Fat: 18g, Carbs: 2g, Protein: 35g, Sugar: 0g, Sodium: 100mg, Potassium: 800mg, Cholesterol: 80mg

SAUTÉED SHRIMP WITH SPINACH

PREPARATION TIME: 10 min

COOKING TIME: 10 min

MODE OF COOKING: Sautéing

SERVINGS: 4

INGREDIENTS:

- 1 lb. shrimp, peeled and deveined
- 2 Tbsp olive oil
- 3 cloves garlic, minced
- 4 cups fresh spinach
- Juice of 1 lemon

DIRECTIONS:

1. Heat olive oil in a large skillet over medium heat.
2. Add minced garlic and sauté for 1 minute.
3. Add shrimp and cook for 3-4 minutes, until pink and opaque.
4. Add fresh spinach and cook until wilted, about 2-3 minutes.
5. Drizzle with lemon juice before serving.

TIPS:

- Serve over pasta or rice for a complete meal.
- Add red pepper flakes for a spicy kick.

N.V.: Calories: 180, Fat: 9g, Carbs: 4g, Protein: 23g, Sugar: 0g, Sodium: 220mg, Potassium: 600mg, Cholesterol: 170mg

Imagine the warm, inviting aromas wafting from a kitchen nestled along the sun-drenched shores of the Mediterranean. Here, meat and poultry are not just food but are part of a rich tapestry of culinary tradition that celebrates both taste and well-being. In the Mediterranean diet, meat dishes are crafted to emphasize balance and quality, often enhanced with herbs, spices, and the simplest yet most flavorful ingredients.

In this chapter, we delve into the succulent world of Mediterranean meat and poultry dishes, each crafted with no more than five key ingredients. Our aim is simplistic elegance the kind that turns a few select items into a feast for the senses. From the tender, olive oil-laced chicken roasted with fragrant rosemary to succulent lamb patties kissed by smoky cumin, these recipes showcase how minimal ingredients can yield maximum flavor.

Mediterranean cuisine respects the integrity of its ingredients, allowing the natural flavors of the meat to stand out, complemented subtly by herbs and spices. This approach not only enriches the dish but also aligns with a healthier lifestyle, focusing on lean proteins prepared in ways that cherish their nutritional value without adding excessive fats or calories.

What's particularly beautiful about these recipes is their inherent versatility. Whether you're preparing a quiet dinner for two or setting the table for a family gathering, the recipes in thi chapter adapt beautifully, proving that simplicity does not compromise sophistication. You will find dishes that cater to both the hurried weekday dinners and the leisurely weekend meals, each recipe a testament to the ease and effectiveness of the Mediterranean way of eating.

As we explore these delicious, easy-to-follow recipes, we embark on a culinary journey that promises to enrich your table with dishes that are as nourishing as they are delightful. Let's embrace the age-old wisdom of Mediterranean cooking and transform the simple act of dining into a wholesome, joyful experience.

LEMON HERB GRILLED CHICKEN

PREPARATION TIME: 10 min

COOKING TIME: 20 min

MODE OF COOKING: Grilling

SERVINGS: 4

INGREDIENTS:

- 4 boneless, skinless chicken breasts
- 2 Tbsp olive oil
- Juice of 1 lemon
- 2 cloves garlic, minced
- 1 Tbsp fresh rosemary, chopped

DIRECTIONS:

1. In a bowl, combine olive oil, lemon juice, minced garlic, and chopped rosemary.
2. Add chicken breasts and coat well with the marinade.
3. Preheat grill to medium-high heat.
4. Grill chicken for 6-7 minutes on each side, until fully cooked.
5. Serve immediately.

TIPS:

- Serve with a side of roasted vegetables or a fresh salad.
- Marinate the chicken for at least 30 minutes for extra flavor.

N.V.: Calories: 220, Fat: 10g, Carbs: 1g, Protein: 28g, Sugar: 0g, Sodium: 90mg, Potassium: 400mg, Cholesterol: 80mg

BALSAMIC GLAZED STEAK

PREPARATION TIME: 10 min

COOKING TIME: 15 min

MODE OF COOKING: Grilling

SERVINGS: 4

INGREDIENTS:

- 4 sirloin steaks
- 2 Tbsp olive oil
- 1/4 cup balsamic vinegar
- 2 cloves garlic, minced
- Fresh basil leaves, chopped

DIRECTIONS:

1. In a bowl, combine olive oil, balsamic vinegar, and minced garlic.
2. Marinate the steaks in the mixture for at least 30 minutes.
3. Preheat grill to medium-high heat.
4. Grill steaks for 5-7 minutes on each side, until desired doneness.
5. Garnish with fresh basil leaves before serving.

TIPS:

- Let steaks rest for a few minutes before slicing.

- Serve with a side of mashed potatoes or grilled vegetables.

N.V.: Calories: 350, Fat: 20g, Carbs: 5g, Protein: 30g, Sugar: 3g, Sodium: 150mg, Potassium: 600mg, Cholesterol: 90mg

GARLIC AND HERB ROASTED LAMB

PREPARATION TIME: 15 min

COOKING TIME: 1 hr.

MODE OF COOKING: Roasting

SERVINGS: 4

INGREDIENTS:

- 1.5 lb. lamb shoulder, boneless
- 2 Tbsp olive oil
- 3 cloves garlic, minced
- 1 Tbsp fresh rosemary, chopped
- Salt and pepper to taste

DIRECTIONS:

1. Preheat oven to 375°F (190°C).
2. In a bowl, combine olive oil, minced garlic, chopped rosemary, salt, and pepper.
3. Rub the mixture all over the lamb shoulder.
4. Place lamb in a roasting pan and roast for 1 hour, or until internal temperature reaches 145°F (63°C).
5. Let rest for 10 minutes before slicing and serving.

TIPS:

- Serve with a side of roasted potatoes or a fresh green salad.
- Add a splash of red wine to the roasting pan for extra flavor.

N.V.: Calories: 350, Fat: 25g, Carbs: 1g, Protein: 30g, Sugar: 0g, Sodium: 120mg, Potassium: 400mg, Cholesterol: 100mg

MEDITERRANEAN CHICKEN SKEWERS

PREPARATION TIME: 15 min

COOKING TIME: 15 min

MODE OF COOKING: Grilling

SERVINGS: 4

INGREDIENTS:

- 1 lb. chicken breast, cut into cubes
- 1 red bell pepper, cut into chunks
- 1 yellow bell pepper, cut into chunks
- 1 red onion, cut into chunks
- 2 Tbsp olive oil

DIRECTIONS:

1. Preheat grill to medium-high heat.
2. Thread chicken, bell peppers, and onion onto skewers.
3. Brush with olive oil and season with salt and pepper.
4. Grill skewers for 5-7 minutes on each side, until chicken is cooked through.
5. Serve immediately.

TIPS:

- Serve with a side of tzatziki sauce or a fresh salad.
- Soak wooden skewers in water for 30 minutes before grilling to prevent burning.

N.V.: Calories: 200, Fat: 10g, Carbs: 5g, Protein: 25g, Sugar: 3g, Sodium: 90mg, Potassium: 400mg, Cholesterol: 80mg

LEMON THYME ROASTED CHICKEN

PREPARATION TIME: 10 min

COOKING TIME: 1 hr.

MODE OF COOKING: Roasting

SERVINGS: 4

INGREDIENTS:

- 1 whole chicken (about 4 lbs.)
- 2 Tbsp olive oil
- Juice of 1 lemon
- 3 cloves garlic, minced
- 1 Tbsp fresh thyme, chopped

DIRECTIONS:

1. Preheat oven to 375°F (190°C).
2. In a bowl, combine olive oil, lemon juice, minced garlic, and chopped thyme.
3. Rub the mixture all over the chicken.
4. Place chicken in a roasting pan and roast for 1 hour, or until internal temperature reaches 165°F (74°C).
5. Let rest for 10 minutes before carving and serving.

TIPS:

- Serve with a side of roasted vegetables or potatoes.
- Baste the chicken with its juices halfway through cooking for extra flavor.

N.V.: Calories: 400, Fat: 28g, Carbs: 1g, Protein: 35g, Sugar: 0g, Sodium: 120mg, Potassium: 400mg, Cholesterol: 120mg

HONEY MUSTARD PORK CHOPS

PREPARATION TIME: 10 min

COOKING TIME: 20 min

MODE OF COOKING: Sautéing

SERVINGS: 4

INGREDIENTS:

- 4 pork chops
- 2 Tbsp olive oil
- 2 Tbsp Dijon mustard
- 2 Tbsp honey
- 2 cloves garlic, minced

DIRECTIONS:

1. In a bowl, combine Dijon mustard, honey, and minced garlic.
2. Brush the mixture over the pork chops.
3. Heat olive oil in a skillet over medium-high heat.
4. Sauté pork chops for 5-6 minutes on each side, until cooked through.
5. Serve immediately.

TIPS:

- Serve with a side of mashed potatoes or steamed vegetables.
- Garnish with fresh thyme or parsley for added flavor.

N.V.: Calories: 300, Fat: 18g, Carbs: 10g, Protein: 25g, Sugar: 8g, Sodium: 300mg, Potassium: 450mg, Cholesterol: 80mg

MEDITERRANEAN BEEF KABOBS

PREPARATION TIME: 15 min

COOKING TIME: 15 min

MODE OF COOKING: Grilling

SERVINGS: 4

INGREDIENTS:

- 1 lb. beef sirloin, cut into cubes
- 1 red bell pepper, cut into chunks
- 1 green bell pepper, cut into chunks
- 1 red onion, cut into chunks
- 2 Tbsp olive oil

DIRECTIONS:

1. Preheat grill to medium-high heat.
2. Thread beef, red bell pepper, green bell pepper, and onion onto skewers.
3. Brush with olive oil and season with salt and pepper.
4. Grill kabobs for 10-12 minutes, turning occasionally, until beef is cooked to desired doneness.
5. Serve immediately.

TIPS:

- Marinate the beef in olive oil, garlic, and lemon juice for extra flavor.
- Serve with a side of tzatziki or hummus.

N.V.: Calories: 250, Fat: 15g, Carbs: 5g, Protein: 25g, Sugar: 2g, Sodium: 70mg, Potassium: 500mg, Cholesterol: 70mg

GARLIC ROSEMARY PORK TENDERLOIN

PREPARATION TIME: 10 min

COOKING TIME: 25 min

MODE OF COOKING: Roasting

SERVINGS: 4

INGREDIENTS:

- 1 lb. pork tenderloin
- 2 Tbsp olive oil
- 3 cloves garlic, minced
- 1 Tbsp fresh rosemary, chopped
- Salt and pepper to taste

DIRECTIONS:

1. Preheat oven to 400°F (200°C).
2. In a bowl, combine olive oil, minced garlic, and chopped rosemary.
3. Rub the mixture over the pork tenderloin and season with salt and pepper.
4. Place pork tenderloin in a roasting pan and roast for 25 minutes, or until internal temperature reaches 145°F (63°C).
5. Let rest for 10 minutes before slicing and serving.

TIPS:

- Serve with roasted potatoes or steamed vegetables.
- Drizzle with a balsamic reduction for added flavor.

N.V.: Calories: 210, Fat: 10g, Carbs: 1g, Protein: 28g, Sugar: 0g, Sodium: 120mg, Potassium: 500mg, Cholesterol: 80mg

LEMON BASIL CHICKEN THIGHS

PREPARATION TIME: 10 min

COOKING TIME: 25 min

MODE OF COOKING: Baking

SERVINGS: 4

INGREDIENTS:

- 4 chicken thighs, bone-in and skin-on
- 2 Tbsp olive oil
- Juice of 1 lemon
- 2 cloves garlic, minced
- Fresh basil leaves, chopped

DIRECTIONS:

1. Preheat oven to 375°F (190°C).
2. In a bowl, combine olive oil, lemon juice, minced garlic, and chopped basil.
3. Rub the mixture over the chicken thighs and place them in a baking dish.
4. Bake for 25 minutes, or until the internal temperature reaches 165°F (74°C).
5. Serve immediately.

TIPS:

- Serve with a side of rice or quinoa.
- Garnish with additional basil leaves for extra freshness.

N.V.: Calories: 300, Fat: 20g, Carbs: 2g, Protein: 26g, Sugar: 0g, Sodium: 90mg, Potassium: 400mg, Cholesterol: 120mg

HERB-CRUSTED LAMB CHOPS

PREPARATION TIME: 10 min

COOKING TIME: 15 min

MODE OF COOKING: Grilling

SERVINGS: 4

INGREDIENTS:

- 8 lamb chops
- 2 Tbsp olive oil
- 3 cloves garlic, minced
- 1 Tbsp fresh thyme, chopped
- Salt and pepper to taste

DIRECTIONS:

1. Preheat grill to medium-high heat.
2. In a bowl, combine olive oil, minced garlic, and chopped thyme.
3. Rub the mixture over the lamb chops and season with salt and pepper.
4. Grill lamb chops for 5-7 minutes on each side, until desired doneness.
5. Serve immediately.

TIPS:

- Serve with a mint yogurt sauce for extra flavor.
- Let lamb chops rest for a few minutes before serving.

N.V.: Calories: 350, Fat: 25g, Carbs: 1g, Protein: 30g, Sugar: 0g, Sodium: 100mg, Potassium: 450mg, Cholesterol: 110mg

BALSAMIC GLAZED CHICKEN BREASTS

PREPARATION TIME: 10 min

COOKING TIME: 20 min

MODE OF COOKING: Sautéing

SERVINGS: 4

INGREDIENTS:

- 4 boneless, skinless chicken breasts
- 2 Tbsp olive oil
- 1/4 cup balsamic vinegar
- 2 cloves garlic, minced
- Fresh basil leaves, chopped

DIRECTIONS:

1. In a bowl, combine olive oil, balsamic vinegar, and minced garlic.
2. Heat a skillet over medium-high heat and add the chicken breasts.
3. Cook for 5-6 minutes on each side, until cooked through.
4. Add the balsamic mixture to the skillet and cook for an additional 2-3 minutes, until the sauce has reduced and thickened.
5. Sprinkle with fresh basil leaves before serving.

TIPS:

- Serve with a side of steamed vegetables or a fresh salad.
- Garnish with lemon slices for added brightness.

N.V.: Calories: 280, Fat: 12g, Carbs: 4g, Protein: 36g, Sugar: 2g, Sodium: 150mg, Potassium: 500mg, Cholesterol: 90mg

MEDITERRANEAN MEATBALLS

PREPARATION TIME: 10 min

COOKING TIME: 20 min

MODE OF COOKING: Baking

SERVINGS: 4

INGREDIENTS:

- 1 lb. ground beef or lamb
- 1/2 cup breadcrumbs
- 2 cloves garlic, minced
- 1 Tbsp fresh parsley, chopped
- 1 egg

DIRECTIONS:

1. Preheat oven to 375°F (190°C).
2. In a large bowl, combine ground beef or lamb, breadcrumbs, minced garlic, chopped parsley, and egg.
3. Mix until well combined and form into meatballs.
4. Place meatballs on a baking sheet and bake for 20 minutes, until cooked through.
5. Serve immediately.

TIPS:

- Serve with tzatziki or a tomato sauce.
- Add grated Parmesan cheese to the mixture for extra flavor.

N.V.: Calories: 250, Fat: 15g, Carbs: 5g, Protein: 25g, Sugar: 1g, Sodium: 200mg, Potassium: 350mg, Cholesterol: 90mg

As the sun dips below the horizon of the Mediterranean, the twilight hour is not just a signal for the end of the day but also a time of sweet anticipation. In every corner of this sun-kissed region, desserts are not merely a course in a meal but a celebration of life's joys and the seasonal gifts of nature. Welcome to the dessert section of our journey, where simplicity meets sophistication in five-ingredient wonders that promise to delight your senses and add a touch of Mediterranean magic to your table.

Imagine the aroma of freshly baked figs mingling with honey, their juices caramelizing at the edges, or the zesty tang of lemon interwoven with the creamy richness of yoghurt, dancing on your palate. These are not just treats; they are stories told through flavors passed down through generations. Here, each recipe is crafted to bring those stories to your kitchen, ensuring that even the busiest days can end with a spoonful of comfort, tradition, and joy.

In this chapter, we strip away the complex layers often associated with gourmet desserts and go back to basics with ingredients that speak for themselves. By focusing on quality and simplicity, you'll find it surprisingly easy to whip up delectable sweets that keep your heart healthy and your taste buds begging for more. From the rustic charm of almond-studded cookies to the elegant simplicity of a peach and basil sorbet, these desserts are designed to be as easy as they are enchanting.

Remember, the essence of the Mediterranean diet lies in its celebration of natural flavors and local ingredients. Each dessert here embraces this philosophy, offering you a taste of Mediterranean warmth, no matter where you are. So, let's turn the page with a promise an invitation to indulge in a sweet symphony of tastes that not only nourish the body but also feed the soul.

7.1 5-INGREDIENT DESSERT RECIPES

HONEY YOGURT PARFAITS

PREPARATION TIME: 10 min

COOKING TIME: 0 min

MODE OF COOKING: No-cook

SERVINGS: 4

INGREDIENTS:

- 2 cups Greek yogurt
- 1/4 cup honey
- 1 cup granola
- 1 cup mixed berries (strawberries, blueberries, raspberries)
- Fresh mint leaves for garnish

DIRECTIONS:

1. In four serving glasses, layer Greek yogurt and honey.
2. Add a layer of granola.
3. Top with mixed berries.
4. Garnish with fresh mint leaves before serving.

TIPS:

- Use local honey for a more authentic flavor.
- Add a sprinkle of cinnamon for extra warmth.

N.V.: Calories: 250, Fat: 6g, Carbs: 40g, Protein: 10g, Sugar: 28g, Sodium: 70mg, Potassium: 300mg, Cholesterol: 10mg

BAKED PEARS WITH HONEY AND ALMONDS

PREPARATION TIME: 10 min

COOKING TIME: 30 min

MODE OF COOKING: Baking

SERVINGS: 4

INGREDIENTS:

- 4 pears, halved and cored
- 1/4 cup honey
- 1/4 cup sliced almonds
- 1 tsp ground cinnamon
- Fresh mint leaves for garnish

DIRECTIONS:

1. Preheat oven to 375°F (190°C).
2. Place pear halves in a baking dish, cut side up.
3. Drizzle honey over the pears and sprinkle with sliced almonds and ground cinnamon.
4. Bake for 30 minutes, until pears are tender.
5. Garnish with fresh mint leaves before serving.

TIPS:

- Serve with a dollop of Greek yogurt for added creaminess.
- Use a mix of pear varieties for different flavors.

N.V.: Calories: 180, Fat: 5g, Carbs: 36g, Protein: 2g, Sugar: 30g, Sodium: 5mg, Potassium: 250mg, Cholesterol: 0mg

---

LEMON OLIVE OIL CAKE

PREPARATION TIME: 15 min

COOKING TIME: 40 min

MODE OF COOKING: Baking

SERVINGS: 8

INGREDIENTS:

- 1 1/2 cups flour
- 1 cup sugar
- 3/4 cup olive oil
- 2 lemons, zested and juiced
- 3 eggs

DIRECTIONS:

1. Preheat oven to 350°F (175°C).
2. In a large bowl, whisk together flour, sugar, and lemon zest.
3. In another bowl, combine olive oil, lemon juice, and eggs.
4. Pour wet ingredients into dry ingredients and mix until just combined.
5. Pour batter into a greased 9-inch cake pan.
6. Bake for 40 minutes, until a toothpick inserted into the center comes out clean.
7. Let cool before serving.

TIPS:

- Dust with powdered sugar before serving for a touch of sweetness.
- Serve with fresh berries on the side.

N.V.: Calories: 300, Fat: 15g, Carbs: 35g, Protein: 4g, Sugar: 20g, Sodium: 20mg, Potassium: 100mg, Cholesterol: 55mg

---

FIG AND HONEY TART

PREPARATION TIME: 15 min

COOKING TIME: 20 min

MODE OF COOKING: Baking

SERVINGS: 6

INGREDIENTS:

- 1 sheet puff pastry
- 1/4 cup honey
- 8 fresh figs, sliced
- 1/4 cup ricotta cheese
- Fresh thyme leaves for garnish

DIRECTIONS:

1. Preheat oven to 400°F (200°C).
2. Roll out puff pastry on a baking sheet.
3. Spread ricotta cheese over the pastry, leaving a 1-inch border.
4. Arrange fig slices over the ricotta cheese.
5. Drizzle with honey and sprinkle with fresh thyme leaves.
6. Bake for 20 minutes, until the pastry is golden and puffed.
7. Serve warm.

TIPS:

- Use a mix of different figs for added texture and flavor.

- Add a sprinkle of sea salt for a sweet-salty contrast.

N.V.: Calories: 250, Fat: 12g, Carbs: 32g, Protein: 4g, Sugar: 15g, Sodium: 150mg, Potassium: 150mg, Cholesterol: 10mg

ALMOND BISCOTTI

PREPARATION TIME: 15 min

COOKING TIME: 30 min

MODE OF COOKING: Baking

SERVINGS: 8

INGREDIENTS:

- 1 1/2 cups flour
- 3/4 cup sugar
- 1/2 cup whole almonds
- 2 eggs
- 1 tsp almond extract

DIRECTIONS:

1. Preheat oven to 350°F (175°C).
2. In a large bowl, mix together flour, sugar, and whole almonds.
3. In another bowl, beat eggs and almond extract.
4. Add wet ingredients to dry ingredients and mix until combined.
5. Divide dough in half and shape into two logs on a baking sheet.
6. Bake for 20 minutes, until firm.
7. Let cool for 10 minutes, then slice into biscotti and bake for another 10 minutes.
8. Let cool completely before serving.

TIPS:

- Dip one end of each biscotti in melted dark chocolate for a decadent touch.

- Store in an airtight container for up to two weeks.

N.V.: Calories: 200, Fat: 7g, Carbs: 30g, Protein: 4g, Sugar: 15g, Sodium: 50mg, Potassium: 100mg, Cholesterol: 35mg

GREEK YOGURT AND HONEY POPSICLES

PREPARATION TIME: 10 min

COOKING TIME: 0 min

FREEZING TIME: 4 hrs.

MODE OF COOKING: Freezing

SERVINGS: 4

INGREDIENTS:

- 2 cups Greek yogurt
- 1/4 cup honey
- 1/2 cup mixed berries
- 1 tsp vanilla extract
- Popsicle sticks

DIRECTIONS:

1. In a bowl, mix Greek yogurt, honey, and vanilla extract.
2. Fold in mixed berries.
3. Pour mixture into popsicle molds and insert sticks.
4. Freeze for at least 4 hours, until solid.
5. Remove from molds and serve.

TIPS:

- Use silicone molds for easy removal.
- Substitute mixed berries with your favorite fruit.

N.V.: Calories: 100, Fat: 2g, Carbs: 18g, Protein: 5g, Sugar: 15g, Sodium: 30mg, Potassium: 150mg, Cholesterol: 10mg

LEMON RICOTTA CHEESECAKE

PREPARATION TIME: 15 min

COOKING TIME: 45 min

MODE OF COOKING: Baking

SERVINGS: 6

INGREDIENTS:

- 1 1/2 cups ricotta cheese
- 1/2 cup honey
- 3 eggs
- Zest of 2 lemons
- Juice of 1 lemon

DIRECTIONS:

1. Preheat oven to 350°F (175°C).
2. In a large bowl, mix ricotta cheese, honey, eggs, lemon zest, and lemon juice until smooth.
3. Pour the mixture into a greased 9-inch springform pan.
4. Bake for 45 minutes, until the cheesecake is set and slightly golden.
5. Let cool before removing from the pan and serving.

TIPS:

- Serve with fresh berries for added flavor.
- Chill the cheesecake in the refrigerator before serving for a firmer texture.

N.V.: Calories: 250, Fat: 12g, Carbs: 25g, Protein: 12g, Sugar: 20g, Sodium: 100mg, Potassium: 200mg, Cholesterol: 120mg

GREEK HONEY WALNUT CAKE

PREPARATION TIME: 15 min

COOKING TIME: 40 min

MODE OF COOKING: Baking

SERVINGS: 8

INGREDIENTS:

- 1 1/2 cups flour
- 1/2 cup honey
- 1/2 cup chopped walnuts
- 1/2 cup olive oil
- 2 eggs

DIRECTIONS:

1. Preheat oven to 350°F (175°C).
2. In a large bowl, mix flour, honey, chopped walnuts, olive oil, and eggs until well combined.
3. Pour the batter into a greased 9-inch cake pan.
4. Bake for 40 minutes, until a toothpick inserted into the center comes out clean.
5. Let cool before serving.

TIPS:

- Drizzle extra honey on top of the cake before serving.
- Serve with a dollop of Greek yogurt for a creamy contrast.

N.V.: Calories: 300, Fat: 18g, Carbs: 35g, Protein: 5g, Sugar: 20g, Sodium: 50mg, Potassium: 150mg, Cholesterol: 35mg

ALMOND AND ORANGE BISCOTTI

PREPARATION TIME: 15 min

COOKING TIME: 30 min

MODE OF COOKING: Baking

SERVINGS: 8

INGREDIENTS:

- 1 1/2 cups flour
- 1/2 cup sugar
- 1/2 cup whole almonds
- 2 eggs
- Zest of 1 orange

DIRECTIONS:

1. Preheat oven to 350°F (175°C).
2. In a large bowl, mix flour, sugar, whole almonds, eggs, and orange zest until combined.
3. Shape the dough into two logs and place on a baking sheet.
4. Bake for 20 minutes, until firm.
5. Let cool for 10 minutes, then slice into biscotti and bake for another 10 minutes.
6. Let cool completely before serving.

TIPS:

- Dip the biscotti in melted chocolate for an extra treat.
- Store in an airtight container for up to two weeks.

N.V.: Calories: 200, Fat: 7g, Carbs: 30g, Protein: 4g, Sugar: 15g, Sodium: 50mg, Potassium: 100mg, Cholesterol: 35mg

GREEK YOGURT WITH FIGS AND HONEY

PREPARATION TIME: 5 min

COOKING TIME: 0 min

MODE OF COOKING: No-cook

SERVINGS: 4

INGREDIENTS:

- 2 cups Greek yogurt
- 1/4 cup honey
- 8 fresh figs, halved
- 1 tsp cinnamon
- Fresh mint leaves for garnish

DIRECTIONS:

1. In serving bowls, divide Greek yogurt.
2. Drizzle honey over the yogurt.
3. Arrange fig halves on top.
4. Sprinkle with cinnamon and garnish with fresh mint leaves.

TIPS:

- Serve with a sprinkle of granola for added crunch.
- Use dried figs if fresh figs are not available.

N.V.: Calories: 150, Fat: 2g, Carbs: 28g, Protein: 7g, Sugar: 20g, Sodium: 50mg, Potassium: 250mg, Cholesterol: 5mg

PISTACHIO AND HONEY BAKLAVA BITES

PREPARATION TIME: 15 min

COOKING TIME: 30 min

MODE OF COOKING: Baking

SERVINGS: 8

INGREDIENTS:

- 1 cup pistachios, chopped
- 1/2 cup honey
- 1/2 cup butter, melted
- 1 tsp cinnamon
- 1 package phyllo dough

DIRECTIONS:

1. Preheat oven to 350°F (175°C).
2. In a bowl, mix chopped pistachios, honey, melted butter, and cinnamon.
3. Layer phyllo dough sheets, brushing each layer with melted butter, and spread the pistachio mixture on top.
4. Roll up and cut into bite-sized pieces.
5. Place on a baking sheet and bake for 30 minutes, until golden and crispy.
6. Drizzle with extra honey before serving.

TIPS:

- Serve with a cup of strong coffee or tea.
- Store in an airtight container to keep them fresh.

N.V.: Calories: 250, Fat: 15g, Carbs: 28g, Protein: 4g, Sugar: 18g, Sodium: 150mg, Potassium: 200mg, Cholesterol: 30mg

DARK CHOCOLATE AND ALMOND CLUSTERS

PREPARATION TIME: 5 min

COOKING TIME: 10 min

MODE OF COOKING: Melting

SERVINGS: 8

INGREDIENTS:

- 1 cup dark chocolate chips
- 1 cup whole almonds
- 1/4 cup dried cranberries
- 1 tsp sea salt
- 1 tsp vanilla extract

DIRECTIONS:

1. Melt dark chocolate chips in a double boiler or microwave until smooth.
2. Stir in whole almonds, dried cranberries, sea salt, and vanilla extract.
3. Drop spoonfuls of the mixture onto a parchment-lined baking sheet.
4. Refrigerate for at least 30 minutes until set.
5. Serve chilled.

TIPS:

- Use a variety of nuts for added texture.
- Sprinkle extra sea salt on top for a salty-sweet contrast.

N.V.: Calories: 180, Fat: 12g, Carbs: 18g, Protein: 3g, Sugar: 14g, Sodium: 60mg, Potassium: 250mg, Cholesterol: 0mg

Volume Measurements

US Measurement	Metric Measurement
1 tsp (tsp)	5 milliliters (ml)
1 tbsp (tbsp)	15 milliliters (ml)
1 fluid ounce (fl oz)	30 milliliters (ml)
1 Cup	240 milliliters (ml)
1 pint (2 Cs)	470 milliliters (ml)
1 quart (4 Cs)	0.95 liters (L)
1 gallon (16 Cs)	3.8 liters (L)

Weight Measurements

US Measurement	Metric Measurement
1 ounce (oz)	28 grams (g)
1 pound (lb)	450 grams (g)
1 pound (lb)	0.45 kilograms (kg)

Length Measurements

US Measurement	Metric Measurement
1 inch (in)	2.54 centimeters (cm)
1 foot (ft)	30.48 centimeters (cm)
1 foot (ft)	0.3048 meters (m)
1 yard (yd)	0.9144 meters (m)

Temperature Conversions

Fahrenheit (°F)	Celsius (°C)
32°F	0°C
212°F	100°C
Formula: (°F - 32) x 0.5556 = °C	Formula: (°C x 1.8) + 32 = °F

Oven Temperature Conversions

US Oven Term	Fahrenheit (°F)	Celsius (°C)
Very Slow	250°F	120°C
Slow	300-325°F	150-165°C
Moderate	350-375°F	175-190°C
Moderately Hot	400°F	200°C
Hot	425-450°F	220-230°C
Very Hot	475-500°F	245-260°C

Embarking on a 30-day exploration of the Mediterranean diet isn't merely about altering what you eat it's about transforming how you feel, function, and flourish over a month of nourishing your body and soul with the simplest, yet most profound flavors the Mediterranean has to offer. This journey is designed to gently integrate the healthful and robust traditions of Mediterranean eating into your daily routine, simplifying mealtime while enriching your palate and health.

As we delve into this 30-day meal plan, imagine each recipe as a brushstroke in a vibrant culinary tapestry, painting a picture of health and ease. Each week, you'll uncover the delights of meals that require minimal ingredients yet deliver maximum flavor think succulent olives paired with crisp cucumbers on a bed of lush greens, or a tender fish fillet kissed by herbs and the zest of a lemon.

The beauty of this plan lies in its flexibility and the ease with which it can be adapted to suit individual tastes and dietary needs. Unlike rigid diet schemes that dictate every morsel, this meal plan encourages you to immerse yourself in the essence of Mediterranean cooking, which celebrates the use of fresh, seasonal ingredients to create meals that are both nutritious and gratifying.

Let's ease the notion that healthy eating is too complicated or time-consuming for our busy lives. Each recipe in the upcoming pages is carefully crafted to ensure that you spend less time in the kitchen but more time savoring and benefiting from each meal. From delectable breakfasts to invigorating dinners, each day unfolds with new dishes to enthuse both seasoned palates and new adventurers alike.

As you transition through the days, take note of the subtle shifts in your energy, your mood, and even your cravings. This is not just about feeding the stomach but nourishing the spirit. Prepare to be rejuvenated, to feel anchored in the practices of Mediterranean living, and inspired by the simplicity of eating well. Welcome to thirty days of heartwarming, easy-to-prepare meals that promise to, step by step, day by day, transform your approach to healthful living.

	breakfast	snack	lunch	snack	dinner
Day 1	Greek Yogurt with Honey and Walnuts	Greek Honey Walnut Cake	Creamy Tomato Basil Soup	Simple tomato bruschetta	Lemon Herb Grilled Chicken
Day 2	Avocado and Egg Toast	Lemon Ricotta Cheesecake	Greek Lemon Chicken Soup	Honey Yogurt Parfaits	Baked Cod with Tomatoes and Olives
Day 3	Tomato and Feta Cheese Omelet	Tahini Sauce with Carrot Sticks	Hearty Lentil Soup	Almond and Orange Biscotti	Garlic and Herb Roasted Lamb
Day 4	Mediterranean Smoothie Bowl	Dark Chocolate and Almond Clusters	Simple Chickpea Soup	Greek Yogurt with Figs and Honey	Mediterranean Tuna Salad
Day 5	Spinach and Feta Stuffed Peppers	Baked Pears with Honey and Almonds	Zucchini and Mint Soup	Lemon Olive Oil Cake	Lemon Thyme Roasted Chicken
Day 6	Banana and Almond Butter Toast	Classic Tzatziki Sauce with Veggies	Roasted Red Pepper Soup	Greek Yogurt and Honey Popsicles	Garlic Butter Shrimp
Day 7	Mediterranean Breakfast Burrito	Almond Biscotti	Tuscan White Bean Soup	Greek Honey Walnut Cake	Mediterranean Beef Kabobs
Day 8	Smoked Salmon and Avocado Toast	Simple tomato bruschetta	Mediterranean Fish Soup	Lemon Ricotta Cheesecake	Lemon Garlic Grilled Mackerel
Day 9	Mediterranean Quinoa Breakfast Bowl	Almond and Orange Biscotti	Carrot and Ginger Soup	Pistachio and Honey Baklava Bites	Lemon Basil Chicken Thighs
Day 10	Ricotta and Honey Toast	Greek Yogurt with Figs and Honey	Spinach and Potato Soup	Tahini Sauce with Carrot Sticks	Herb-Crusted Cod

	breakfast	snack	lunch	snack	dinner
Day 11	Mediterranean Egg Muffins	Classic Tzatziki Sauce with Veggies	Mediterranean Lentil and Spinach Soup	Baked Pears with Honey and Almonds	Balsamic Glazed Chicken Breasts
Day 12	Mediterranean Breakfast Salad	Greek Yogurt and Honey Popsicles	Red Lentil and Tomato Soup	Fig and Honey Tart	Sautéed Shrimp with Spinach
Day 13	Greek Yogurt with Honey and Walnuts	Greek Honey Walnut Cake	Greek Salad	Almond Biscotti	Lemon Herb Grilled Chicken
Day 14	Avocado and Egg Toast	Olive Tapenade with Crackers	Caprese Salad	Honey Yogurt Parfaits	Baked Cod with Tomatoes and Olives
Day 15	Tomato and Feta Cheese Omelet	Pistachio and Honey Baklava Bites	Mediterranean Quinoa Salad	Almond and Orange Biscotti	Garlic and Herb Roasted Lamb
Day 16	Mediterranean Smoothie Bowl	Dark Chocolate and Almond Clusters	Cucumber and Mint Salad	Classic Tzatziki Sauce with Veggies	Mediterranean Tuna Salad
Day 17	Spinach and Feta Stuffed Peppers	Baked Pears with Honey and Almonds	Arugula and Parmesan Salad	Lemon Olive Oil Cake	Lemon Thyme Roasted Chicken
Day 18	Banana and Almond Butter Toast	Fig and Honey Tart	Mediterranean Chickpea Salad	Greek Yogurt and Honey Popsicles	Garlic Butter Shrimp
Day 19	Mediterranean Breakfast Burrito	Almond Biscotti	Watermelon and Feta Salad	Simple tomato bruschetta	Mediterranean Beef Kabobs
Day 20	Smoked Salmon and Avocado Toast	Honey Yogurt Parfaits	Roasted Beet and Orange Salad	Lemon Ricotta Cheesecake	Lemon Garlic Grilled Mackerel

	breakfast	snack	lunch	snack	dinner
Day 21	Mediterranean Quinoa Breakfast Bowl	Tahini Sauce with Carrot Sticks	Panzanella Salad	Pistachio and Honey Baklava Bites	Lemon Basil Chicken Thighs
Day 22	Ricotta and Honey Toast	Greek Yogurt with Figs and Honey	Avocado and Tomato Salad	Dark Chocolate and Almond Clusters	Herb-Crusted Cod
Day 23	Mediterranean Egg Muffins	Lemon Olive Oil Cake	Mediterranean Farro Salad	Baked Pears with Honey and Almonds	Balsamic Glazed Chicken Breasts
Day 24	Mediterranean Breakfast Salad	Classic Tzatziki Sauce with Veggies	Spinach and Strawberry Salad	Fig and Honey Tart	Sautéed Shrimp with Spinach
Day 25	Greek Yogurt with Honey and Walnuts	Greek Honey Walnut Cake	Creamy Tomato Basil Soup	Almond Biscotti	Lemon Herb Grilled Chicken
Day 26	Avocado and Egg Toast	Olive Tapenade with Crackers	Greek Lemon Chicken Soup	Honey Yogurt Parfaits	Baked Cod with Tomatoes and Olives
Day 27	Tomato and Feta Cheese Omelet	Pistachio and Honey Baklava Bites	Hearty Lentil Soup	Almond and Orange Biscotti	Garlic and Herb Roasted Lamb
Day 28	Mediterranean Smoothie Bowl	Dark Chocolate and Almond Clusters	Simple Chickpea Soup	Greek Yogurt with Figs and Honey	Mediterranean Tuna Salad
Day 29	Spinach and Feta Stuffed Peppers	Simple tomato bruschetta	Zucchini and Mint Soup	Tahini Sauce with Carrot Sticks	Lemon Thyme Roasted Chicken
Day 30	Banana and Almond Butter Toast	Fig and Honey Tart	Roasted Red Pepper Soup	Greek Yogurt and Honey Popsicles	Garlic Butter Shrimp

CONCLUSION

As we approach the end of our journey through the vibrant flavors and timeless traditions of the Mediterranean diet, it's important to pause and reflect on the transformative path we've explored together. Embracing the Mediterranean lifestyle isn't merely about changing what's on your plate; it's about altering your approach to eating for health, for longevity, and for joy.

Throughout this book, we've uncovered how simple ingredients can weave together to create dishes that not only nourish the body but also delight the senses. It's been an adventure of rediscovery, seeing how a diet rich in vegetables, fruits, lean proteins, and heart-healthy fats can influence not just our physical health but our overall quality of life. The Mediterranean diet isn't just a fleeting wellness trend but a heritage, passed down through generations, proven by science to benefit our hearts, minds, and souls.

And now, as you stand on the threshold of continuing your Mediterranean journey, remember that the essence of this diet is rooted in simplicity and pleasure. Whether it was the tangy zest of a lemon enhancing a delicate fish or the robust taste of olive oil transforming a salad, each recipe was designed to bring ease and delight to your kitchen.

Let us not forget the practical steps we've shared minimizing kitchen time without sacrificing flavor, making smart and sustainable choices in our ingredients, and adapting traditional dishes to fit our hectic modern lives. These elements are crucial as they empower you to maintain this healthful path.

In embracing the Mediterranean way, you've embraced a life where eating is an act of caring for yourself, your loved ones, and the environment. Carry forward this spirit, letting the flavors of the Mediterranean fill your meals with both health and happiness.

Emboldened by the benefits of this diet and the beauty of its simplicity, may you continue to find joy in every meal and pride in every dish. Here's to your vibrant journey forward, infused with good food, great health, and boundless vitality.

RECAP OF THE MEDITERRANEAN DIET BENEFITS

Throughout our pages dripping with the aroma of garlic, zestiness of olives, and robustness of whole grains, we have witnessed how the Mediterranean diet, a culinary treasure trove esteemed globally, benefits every dimension of wellness. Embodying much more than a mere nutritional guideline, it encompasses a lifestyle celebrated for its profound impacts on longevity and vitality. It is no coincidence that regions nestling this way of eating, like Crete and Sardinia, are homes to some of the world's most vibrant, healthiest populations.

The virtue of the Mediterranean diet lies in its ability to meld sheer pleasure and health convivial family meals, fresh, flavorful ingredients, and a balance that scoffs at the rigid restrictions championed by fad diets. Instead, it's a graceful dance of moderation, variety, and natural wholesomeness.

Starting with heart health, the linchpin of numerous studies, the Mediterranean diet emerges as a beacon of hope. Rich in heart-healthy fats from olive oil, nuts, and seeds, it's shown to significantly reduce the risk of cardiovascular disease. These fats don't just lower bad cholesterol; they are potent warriors battling inflammation a less visible, yet perilous, foe within our arteries. Then, there are the fish, brimming with omega-3 fatty acids, a blessing for heart rhythm and vascular health. It's like each meal is a comforting hug to the heart, nurturing its rhythm and ensuring its strength.

The benefits ripple broader and deeper, touching on maladies like diabetes and obesity. High in dietary fiber from an abundance of fruits, vegetables, and whole grains, the diet stabilizes blood sugar and fosters a healthy weight. Fiber does not merely fill it satiates and slows the absorption of glucose, which spells harmonized energy levels and moods throughout the day. Additionally, the moderate consumption of wine, especially red, underlines a principle innate to Mediterranean drinking habits: indulgence in moderation, enjoyed with meals enhancing the sociable, leisurely mealtime pace that also helps in tempering the day's stresses.

From the neurological corridors of our health, the Mediterranean diet's influence is equally persuasive. Emerging research lauds its ability to fend off cognitive decline associated with aging. The nutrient-dense staples of the diet leafy greens, berries, nuts are loaded with antioxidants and vitamins that curtain our neural paths against oxidative stress and inflammation, playing a significant role in maintaining cognitive function and potentially lowering the risk of neurodegenerative diseases like Alzheimer's and Parkinson's. Each meal thus weaves a protective web around our treasured memories and cognitive capacities.

But it's not just about the physical. The diet casts a glow on mental health, too. By encouraging a diet punctuated with unprocessed foods, rich in fruits and vegetables, and low in meat and dairy, it aligns with nutritional patterns associated with reduced incidences of depression and anxiety. The linkage isn't coincidental food influences mood-regulating neurotransmitters within the brain while the ritual of preparing and enjoying wholesome meals can act as a mindful respite from the noise of life's hustle.

Moreover, the inherent encouragement of communal eating boosts psychological well-being by bolstering social bonds an often-overlooked aspect of health. The Mediterranean way makes th dining table a place of reunion, conversation, and shared joy, fostering a sense of belonging and emotional contentment.

As we consider the broader implications, it's evident the diet also respects the earth the very source of its bounty. Seasonality, sustainability, and local sourcing are pillars that not only ensure the lowest carbon footprint but also the highest degree of nutrient retention in foods. This harmonious relationship with nature is perhaps why the diet has sustained through centuries, a testament to its inherent respect for the environment.

Embracing the Mediterranean way means more than enjoying delicious meals it's about participating in a sustainable, health-promoting lifestyle that cherishes the abundance of nature's larder, respects our bodies, and celebrates our communal humanity. You are not just feeding your body; you are nurturing your spirit, delighting your senses, and taking part in an age-old, ever-evolving tradition of wellness.

This way of life, this dietary culture, offers a blueprint for a healthful, joyous existence that is both timeless and astonishingly simple. With every dish prepared, with every meal enjoyed, you're not just sustaining your body; you are preserving a cultural heritage and fostering an environment where well-being thrives. Through the Mediterranean diet, we find that the most enduring form of beauty is good health, and the surest path to happiness is to live in sync with the natural world. In this way, the Mediterranean diet transcends the bounds of nutritional science to touch every facet of life, offering a comprehensive blueprint for a robust, joyful existence.

ENCOURAGEMENT FOR CONTINUED HEALTHY EATING

Embarking on the path of the Mediterranean diet is not just about adopting a set of recipes; it's about embracing a lifestyle that promotes richness in flavor and health. Having ventured through the myriad benefits and the joyous meals that the Mediterranean kitchen offers, the road ahead is full of both promise and ongoing commitment. But even the most picturesque journeys can have their challenges, and it is essential to embrace continuous motivation to maintain and uphold this wholesome way of life.

The Mediterranean lifestyle is as much about enjoying the diversity of food as it is about balancing the mind, body, and spirit. To tread this path continuously requires a mindset that celebrates each meal as an opportunity for nourishment and delight. As you might have noticed, these are not just meals; they are invitations to explore, to taste, and to relish life's simple pleasures. The beauty of this diet lies not in restriction but in its abundant variety, which prevents the culinary fatigue often associated with more prescriptive diets.

A practical step in nurturing this newfound eating habit is to remember the art of moderation and variation, core pillars of the Mediterranean diet that stood the test of time. The act of changing your eating habits should not feel like a herculean task but more like a natural transition into making better choices every day. Just as a single drop creates ripples in water, each small, healthy choice contributes to a larger pattern of benefits.

One sustainable way to nurture this journey is to weave the diet into the fabric of your routine. This might mean starting with incorporating more fruits and vegetables into your meals, choosing whole grains over processed alternatives, or replacing butter with olive oil. Small shifts can lead to profound changes. Just like the soothing Mediterranean breeze, let these changes be gentle but impactful.

Moreover, consider the vibrant social aspect of the Mediterranean lifestyle. Meals are more than sustenance; they are a communal celebration. Try to make mealtime a shared experience, as this enhances not only how you eat but also why you eat. Sharing a table with loved ones not only satisfies the stomach but also the soul, enriching the overall dining experience and reinforcing the joy and connection found in healthy eating.

Another valuable encouragement is to continuously educate oneself about the foods and culture of the Mediterranean. Understanding the origins and benefits of different ingredients can deepen your appreciation for them and inspire you to use them creatively. Remember, innovation is at the heart of Mediterranean kitchens, where traditional recipes have evolved over centuries, adapting to new tastes and times while maintaining their core nutritional philosophies.

It's crucial, too, to listen to your body. Recognize how different foods impact your wellbeing, adjusting as necessary to accommodate what makes you feel the most vibrant and alive. This diet encourages tuning into your physical responses to meals, promoting an internal awareness that goes beyond eating for pleasure alone.

If challenges arise, be they from dietary monotony or external pressures, rekindle your motivation by recalling the health benefits you're fostering. Visualize the positive changes the enhanced energy, the better health markers, and the general wellbeing you experience. Let these successes, no matter how small, fuel your journey forward.

At times when your resolve might waver, draw strength from the Mediterranean's timeless wisdom Good health is a life-long banquet to be enjoyed one bite at a time. You are not just eating; you are crafting a legacy of health that can influence generations to come. Each choice to eat well is a vote for your future a future filled with zest, vigor, and the joy of living well.

Lastly, keep the conversation going whether with friends, online, or in your community. Sharing your journey, exchanging ideas, and celebrating milestones can fortify your commitment and inspire others. This diet thrives on the joy of sharing, not just meals but experiences and successes. By now, you know that the Mediterranean diet is more than just a checklist of foods to eat. It's a narrative of cultures, histories, and landscapes rich with beauty and taste. It's a dialogue between tradition and innovation, weaving past with present in every bite. May this journey nurture not just your body but also your heart and spirit, as you continue to savor and celebrate the abundant flavors of the Mediterranean, meal by meal.

ADDITIONAL RESOURCES AND READING

As you continue to nurture and develop your journey with the Mediterranean diet, the wealth of resources available to deepen your understanding and enhance your cooking practices grows ever richer. While this book aims to serve as a comprehensive guide to both the novice and the adept cook in the art of Mediterranean living, delving into additional resources can provide new perspectives and add depth to your culinary exploration.

Books that delve into the science and joy behind the Mediterranean lifestyle can be wonderfully enlightening. For a deeper understanding of how Mediterranean dietary habits influence longevity and wellbeing, consider *"The Blue Zones Kitchen"* by Dan Buettner, which offers research-backed insights into the diets of the world's longest-lived populations, many of whom thrive on Mediterranean-style eating patterns. This book not only broadens your understanding but also connects you with stories of people around the globe who are thriving on similar diets.

If the science behind the diet fascinates you, *"The Mediterranean Diet for Beginners"* by Rockridge Press provides a straightforward, practical entry to the clinical benefits and how-tos of the lifestyle. This type of reading can arm you with the facts and figures that might prove motivating when implementing this diet in your daily life and discussing it within your social circles.

For those who dream of the vibrant Mediterranean landscapes and cultural richness, books like *"Under the Tuscan Sun"* by Frances Mayes might not be traditional cooking or diet books, but they capture the essence of Mediterranean living its rhythms, ethos, and the zest for life that naturally supports healthful eating habits.

Podcasts, too, are modern gateways to learning and can be a wonderful accompaniment to your cooking. Try listening to episodes from *"The Mediterranean Diet Podcast"* hosted by dietitians and chefs who frequently discuss tips, recipes, and the latest research about the

Mediterranean diet. Engaging in this form of learning can be both casual and educational, enriching your cooking experience without feeling burdensome.

Online forums and platforms can be treasure troves of recipes, advice, and support from like-minded individuals. Websites like the *"Oldways Mediterranean Foods Alliance"* offer a plethora of resources including shopping lists, meal plans, and detailed information about the fundamental ingredients that make Mediterranean cuisine both healthful and delicious. Engaging with an online community can also provide encouragement and inspiration, making your dietary practice feel more like a shared cultural experience rather than a solitary endeavor.

For a visually inspiring journey through the Mediterranean world, the documentary *"Forks Over Knives"* (which explores the benefits of a plant-based diet, aligning closely with Mediterranean dietary principles) can be found on various streaming platforms. The visual celebration of food, combined with compelling evidence on its impacts, can be incredibly motivational.

Local cooking classes can also be an invaluable resource. Immersing yourself in a hands-on learning experience guided by knowledgeable chefs who specialize in Mediterranean cuisine can transform your cooking from following recipes to creating culinary art. These classes often offer more than just cooking techniques; they delve into the whys of ingredient selection and pairing, which can elevate your meals from simple to spectacular.

Lastly, don't underestimate the value of traveling, if possible, to Mediterranean countries. Experiencing the diet within its cultural context provides unparalleled insight. If travel is not an option, local cultural festivals and Mediterranean eateries can also offer authentic experiences closer to home.

Remember, the journey to incorporating the Mediterranean style into your life is not a linear one, nor is it the same for everyone. Each resource you engage with may open new paths in your culinary and lifestyle journey. The beauty of this diet is that it is adaptable and enjoyable true to the spirit of Mediterranean living, where flexibility and pleasure meet health and tradition.

As you explore these resources, let each new learning not overwhelm but inspire you. With each step, each meal, and each story, you're weaving a richer tapestry of well-being that can support not just a healthier body, but a more fulfilled life. Enjoy the journey, for each moment along this path is an opportunity to celebrate living in its most vibrant form.

In the dance of the kitchen, where spoon meets bowl, where the sizzle of olive oil whispers tales of the old world, and where flavors bloom like flowers in spring, gratitude sways through the air, as essential as the ingredients themselves. As we draw the curtains on this culinary adventure, my heart brims over with immense gratitude a tapestry woven from countless threads of support, mentorship, and camaraderie.

Firstly, a deep and heartfelt thank you goes to the wise and spirited grandmothers and grandfathers of the Mediterranean. Their hands, wrinkled and warm from the sun, have kneaded tradition and taste into the very dough of their existence. Their stories and recipes have not just survived; they have thrived, crossing oceans and generations. From them, we learn the essence of the Mediterranean lifestyle that food is more than sustenance; it is memory, it is love, it is community.

To the diligent farmers, fishers, and artisans who nurture, harvest, and craft the olive oil producers who treat every olive with reverence, the vineyard keepers who watch over their vines with the patience of saints, and the market vendors who sell their goods with pride and smiles I am eternally indebted. Their dedication to quality is what builds the foundation of everything the Mediterranean diet stands for. Without their hard work, the authenticity and quality that are hallmarks of this incredible diet would not be possible.

Acknowledgments are also due to the myriad researchers and academics whose tireless work in nutrition and health provides the backbone of understanding that supports this diet. Their studies do more than just validate ancient wisdom; they offer a bridge between tradition and modernity, proving that the old ways, the connected, nature-intertwined ways, have enduring power in our fast-paced world.

A special note of thanks goes to my culinary mentors and peers those seasoned chefs and enthusiastic novices alike, whose passion for Mediterranean cuisine is contagious. Each shared recipe and technique has been a building block in the fortress of knowledge that this book stands on. Their creativity and innovation continue to inspire and push the boundaries of traditional Mediterranean cooking into the realms of global gastronomy.

To my literary agent and editor, whose keen eyes and thoughtful insights have molded this manuscript into something far greater than I could have achieved alone, thank you. Your guidance has been a lighthouse in the occasionally stormy seas of writing and publishing. Likewise, the entire team behind the scenes deserves applause for their commitment to bringing this project to life from the designers who created beautiful pages to the marketing professionals who help share this journey with the world.

Gratitude extends to friends and family whose everyday insights and encouragements have been nothing short of nourishing to the soul. It is one thing to write about food, it is another to live it, and you are the ones who have sampled, savored, and celebrated every step of this flavorful voyage with me.

And, of course, to you, the readers who have embarked on this journey with an open heart and a curious palate. Your eagerness to explore new tastes and incorporate healthy, joyous eating into your life is the ultimate reward for a writer. Every email, comment, and shared story of your culinary adventures fuels my passion and commitment to continue this path.

Lastly, I am grateful for the sun, sea, and soil of the Mediterranean nature's gifts that make this diet deeply nourishing and inherently sustainable. To the waters and lands that give us the bounteous fruits, vegetables, and grains, we owe our continued health and pleasure.

As we close this chapter, know that the book may end but the journey does not. Every meal is an opportunity to cultivate health, enjoy the moment, and connect with others. May your kitchens always be filled with the aromas of joy and the flavors of wellness. Thank you for allowing me to be a part of your culinary exploration into the heart of the Mediterranean. Let us continue to cook, to learn, and to grow together in this delicious pursuit of life well-lived.

YOUR JOURNEY FORWARD

Embarking on the Mediterranean diet is akin to setting sail on a vibrant sea of experiences, where each meal is a discovery and every dish tells a story. As you journey forward with the lessons and flavors of the Mediterranean lifestyle, remember that the path is not merely about following recipes but about embracing a broader philosophy that enhances your connection to food, family, and health.

Think of your kitchen as an ongoing experiment, a laboratory of flavors where traditional ingredients meet your personal flair. Continue to explore the nuances of Mediterranean ingredients how the sharpness of a fresh lemon can elevate a simple fish dish, or how a sprinkle of aromatic herbs can transform a tray of roasted vegetables. Allow yourself the freedom to tweak recipes to your taste, to substitute herbs for what's available in your garden, or to use locally produced cheeses instead of those from distant shores. This flexibility is not just a convenience; it is at the heart of the Mediterranean way, embracing the seasonal and regional, celebrating what is available and at its peak.

Yet, the journey of incorporating the Mediterranean diet into your life extends beyond your dining table. It's about cultivating an understanding of nutrition and its impacts on your body and mind. Engage with the latest nutrition science, and be open to how contemporary research can enhance traditional wisdom. Staying informed will not only help you make better choices but also deepen your appreciation for this age-old, yet ever-evolving, dietary heritage.

Moreover, consider the broader implications of your food choices. The Mediterranean lifestyle is deeply rooted in principles of sustainability and respect for the earth. Each decision to choose local, seasonal produce or to reduce meat consumption can be a step toward a more sustainable future. These choices echo the Mediterranean tradition of living in harmony with the landscape a practice that nourishes both the earth and its inhabitants.

Remember, too, the social component of the Mediterranean diet. Meals are meant to be shared, savored together with family and friends. Make dining an occasion, a time to disconnect from the bustle of modern life and engage in meaningful conversations. In many Mediterranean cultures, preparing and enjoying food is a communal activity that strengthens bonds and nurtures relationships. Extend this tradition to your own table, inviting friends to cook together, or sharing a meal with a neighbor. Through these shared experiences, the principles of the diet weave deeper into the fabric of daily life, enhancing its joys and communal blessings.

As you move forward, let the Mediterranean diet be a canvas for innovation. The principles of the diet are guides, not rules. Innovate dishes that respect these principles while tailoring to contemporary, perhaps busier, lifestyles. Embrace technology and new cooking techniques that can help streamline meal preparation without sacrificing the diet's nutritional integrity.

Be patient with your progress. Changing dietary habits is like learning a new language; it takes time and practice. Celebrate your successes, no matter how small, and learn from the setbacks. Perhaps today, you chose a whole grain bread, or maybe this week, you cooked fish twice. These victories, though seemingly small, are the building blocks of lasting change.

And finally, keep the spirit of adventure alive in your culinary quests. Travel through recipes, exploring the diverse cuisines within the Mediterranean basin from the hearty stews of Morocco to the spice-laden dishes of Turkey, to the olive-oil rich pastas of Italy. Each region offers a unique palette of flavors, techniques, and historical stories that can enrich your cooking and dining experience.

Your journey forward with the Mediterranean diet is not just about maintaining a way of eating but about continuing a way of living a life that celebrates good food, good health, and good company. Carry forward this adventure with curiosity and passion, and let the Mediterranean sun shine on your table, brightening each meal with the joy and health it embodies. Engage with the world around you through its cuisines, embrace change and growth in your diet and lifestyle, and continue to share the bounty of this beautiful eating tradition with those you love.

Flavors of the Sun - The Complete Guide to the Mediterranean Diet for a Healthy Life

Scan qr code to Download SHOPPING LIST PDF

Made in United States
North Haven, CT
21 December 2024

63262477R00063